Martin Walker

THE COLD WAR

And the Making of the Modern World

VINTAGE

First published in Vintage 1994

4 6 8 10 9 7 5 3

Copyright © Walker & Watson 1993

The right of Martin Walker to be identified as the author
of this work has been asserted by him in accordance
with the Copyright, Designs and Patents Act, 1988.

This book is sold subject to the condition that it shall not,
by way of trade or otherwise, be lent, resold, hired out,
or otherwise circulated without the publisher's prior consent
in any form of binding or cover other than that in which it is
published and without a similar condition including this
condition being imposed on the subsequent purchaser.

First published in Great Britain
by Fourth Estate Ltd 1993

Arrow Books Limited
Random House, 20 Vauxhall Bridge Road, London SW1V 2SA

Random House Australia (Pty) Limited
16 Dalmore Drive, Scoresby, Victoria 3179, Australia

Random House New Zealand Limited
18 Poland Road, Glenfield
Auckland 10, New Zealand

Random House South Africa (Pty) Limited
PO Box 2263, Rosebank 2121, South Africa

Random House UK Limited Reg. No. 954009

A CIP catalogue record for this book
is available from the British Library

Papers used by Random House UK Limited
are natural, recyclable products made from wood grown in
sustainable forests. The manufacturing processes conform to
the environmental regulations of the country of origin

ISBN 0 09 913511 6

Printed and bound in Great Britain by
Cox & Wyman Ltd, Reading, Berkshire

Contents

What does this sudden uneasiness mean,
and this confusion? (How grave the faces have become!)
Why are the streets and squares rapidly emptying,
and why is everyone going back home so lost in thought?

Because it is night and the barbarians have not come.
And some men have arrived from the frontiers
and they say that barbarians don't exist any longer.

And now what will become of us without barbarians?
They were a kind of solution.

C. P. Cavafy, 'Waiting for the Barbarians'

Preface

This book is the story of its author's life. I was born into the crucial winter of the Cold War, when the blizzards which devastated the Europe of early 1947 forced the dispatch of a plaintive but historic appeal to Washington. The Durham coalfields near my birthplace, just decorated with the defiant signposts, 'These pits now belong to the People', had frozen solid, along with the nation's railroads and the docks. Six million men, almost a third of the workforce, were laid off. Although nominally a time of peace, the rationing of food was more severe than it had been at the height of Hitler's unrestricted submarine warfare. Exhausted by war, impoverished by peace, Britain belatedly acknowledged that the burden of Empire and of Europe's defence was no longer to be borne, and asked the Americans to take over the support of Greece and Turkey.

It was to be a long mission. I was just starting to toddle when the American atomic bombers were first stationed in Britain. My elder daughter will soon be old enough to have children of her own, and the bombers are still there, along with the American troops on the Rhine. As Senator Pat Moynihan once observed, 'This is the stuff of Roman legions.'

The Cold War has been the constant, implacable condition of the vast demographic wave of the children who were born as the soldiers of World War Two came home to a bitter, uncertain peace. Now that we think it is over, and that the nuclear shadow may at last be passing, and that two members of that generation are now President and Vice-President of the last and lonely superpower, we have to make sense of what the Cold War has been, and how it has shaped us and the uncertain new world ahead, and what it has left behind.

By accidents of geography, of nationality, and then of profession, I find that a remarkable portion of my life has been spent as a curious and usually bewildered non-combatant in the various parts of the Cold War's far-flung front lines. My first memory of a newspaper is reading an account of the mistreatment of British prisoners of war in the Korean conflict. In 1956, at a primary school in the north of England, I published my first newspaper, a rude wall-poster whose headline dealt with the Suez crisis. I remember the prime minister Harold Macmillan visiting my grammar school just after his return from a summit with Nikita Khrushchev in Moscow, and recall my disappointment that he was not wearing the white fur Cossack's hat in which he had looked most dashing in the newspapers. In the Cuban missile crisis of 1962, I took part in my first school debate, arguing with adolescent passion that the Americans must withdraw their missiles from Turkey to save Britain from annihilation.

And yet it seemed natural that, with a father and four uncles who had served in the Royal Air Force during what we still call 'the war', I should join the RAF section of the Cadet Corps, wear a boy-sized uniform each Friday, undergo my pilot's training and accept the duty of being liable to serve as a reservist in time of war. Military service seemed inevitable, part of the condition of a nation that was constantly ready to stand to arms. The odd contradiction of attending Ban the Bomb marches while learning how to fly through the RAF, and making my first visit to the USA through a Nato scholarship for young air cadets, caused no anguish. Opinions were one thing: the reality of national readiness was quite another.

My first visit to the Soviet Union was made in the Easter vacation of 1968, part of a National Union of Students tour. It took us through West Berlin at the time of the Rudi Dutschke riots, through Warsaw as the students battled the security police by the Copernicus statue, and to Moscow and Leningrad where we found Russian students much like ourselves. And so were the students of Prague, thrilling to that extraordinary Spring which spoke of Socialism with a human face, and the students of Paris at their barricades. It was only later, at demonstrations against the Vietnam War at Harvard and in Washington in 1969 and 1970, that I came to understand the self-indulgence of us Western Europeans, not faced with the threat of conscription into an odious war which faced the Americans, and the different but grim menace of civilian life which loomed over my Polish and Russian friends.

It was in that realisation – that the Western Europeans who had begun after 1945 as the Cold War's hostages and had by the late 1960s become its beneficiaries – that this book had its origins. My profession as a journalist has provided endless opportunities to study the Cold War's erratic progress at close hand. Covering the Portuguese revolution of 1974, where a Nato ally seemed for a moment to be tottering into the socialist camp, the strange absence of Soviet influence and aid for an enthusiastic Communist Party emerging from the underground helped explain the superpower stasis which had been agreed for Europe. Just as the West had not moved to the relief of Hungary in 1956, of Czechoslovakia in 1968, of Poland in 1970 and 1981, the Soviets did not exert themselves as Portugal and Spain hauled themselves from their fascist past.

In 1979, newly married and on an extended honeymoon, my wife and I found ourselves in Iran as the Ayatollah's rule consolidated, and then in Afghanistan. We drove from Pakistan through the Quetta Pass to Herat, which had just been retaken after a burst of liberation which had seen a hundred Soviet military advisers and their families slaughtered, and their heads paraded through the town on pikes. In Kabul, the night sky was electric with the tracers of the gunships. The Khalq and Parcham factions of the Afghan Communist Party were at war, the Soviet advisers were joining in, and I had to defy the curfew to chase down some bottled water for my wife, stricken with dysentery. We left through the Khyber Pass on the last civilian convoy.

But not for the first or the last time, I confronted the terrifying irony that while my press card and passport paraded my neutrality, my skin made me indistinguishable from a hated Russian – or in other places at other times, from an equally loathed American imperialist. At a road block in southern Ethiopia in 1975, just after the fall of Haile Selassie, my harmless library card for the British Museum reading room, which carried no name but only some ominous colour-coded symbols, almost got me shot as an American spy. Dodging Moroccan armoured columns with the Polisario guerrillas of the Western Sahara in 1977, or being held at gunpoint by Colonel Gadafy's troops in Libya in 1981, the role of the Cold War proxies of the Third World was brought sharply home. We were all white outsiders, trying to impose our will, or our order, on places where the locals found our presence unwelcome.

Then in Brazil to make sense of the Latin American debt crisis, the awesome, unfolding powers and vulnerabilities of global finance began to grip my imagination in a way that has never ceased. Covering the travails of the Mitterrand government in France in 1983, as a leading European power tried for the last time to enact a programme of social reform in defiance of the economic orthodoxies, the new power of the global market to override the measures for which electorates had voted became bluntly clear. In the following year, I was asked to reopen the *Guardian* bureau in Moscow, and found myself covering not only the peaceful revolution of Perestroika, but the inability of even a centrally planned autarky to escape the disciplines of this global economic system.

As we left Moscow, the Soviet foreign ministry spokesman, the urbane and affable Gennady Gerasimov, who had served as a correspondent in New York, bade me farewell, raised a glass and toasted my departure 'from one declining superpower to the other'. To have covered both Moscow and Washington during the long drawing down of the Cold War has been an extraordinary privilege, and profound thanks are due to Peter Preston, the editor of the *Guardian*, and all my colleagues at that newspaper. The *Guardian* was founded in 1821, as the voice of the booming new industrial city of Manchester. Its birth in the first industrial revolution, its dependence on the first multinational trading system which developed around cotton, may explain why this book is not simply a diplomatic history, but ranges far beyond the usual structures of power and alliances to explore the underlying tectonic shifts in the world's economic system.

Acknowledgements are also due to a number of other organisations and publications which allowed me to explore my developing theories about the Cold War as history. The distinguished American diplomat Bill Maynes, whom I first knew when we were both Congressional fellows of the American Political Science Association, working on Capitol Hill in 1971, has been an outstanding editor of *Foreign Policy*. He and Tom Omestad encouraged me to write on America's role in the world for that august quarterly. Mr Sherle Schwenninger has been a splendid editor of *World Policy Journal*, and maintained a sprightly liberal tradition in American thinking about foreign affairs, in spite of the prolonged intellectual hegemony of conservatism and *realpolitik*. I am grateful to them, and to Mr Peter Doyle and Robert Guttman of *Europe* magazine, the publication of the European Community in the United States, who asked me to explore some of the longer-range implications of the world after the Cold War.

Both the International Press Institute and the Committee to Protect Journalists invited me to return to Moscow for conferences and research trips which proved more than useful. The new journal *Demokratizatsiya*, produced jointly by Moscow State and the American University, invited me on to their editorial board and to chair some of the sessions on democratising the KGB. This resulted in a detailed advisory memorandum for President Boris Yeltsin and, for this book, some unusual insights into the role of intelligence in the Cold War.

Thanks are also due to the Canadian Institute for International Peace and Security and the Czechoslovak Institute for International Relations in Prague, and to Canada's Parliamentary Committee for

Foreign Affairs, who invited me to give papers on European security after the Cold War, some themes of which found their way into this book. I am also grateful to Dr Michael Hogan, editor of *Diplomatic History*, for inviting me to concentrate my thoughts on the latest flurry of books in the newly emerging field of post-Cold War studies.

There has been in recent years a golden age of contemporary history studies in US–Soviet relations and in the Cold War, as archives creak open, memoirs are published, and an entire generation of gifted scholar–journalists has been unleashed. The notes to this book record my debt, and the debt of anyone writing in this field, to Richard Barnet, Dr Michael Beschloss, Kai Bird, Sid Blumenthal, Abe Brumberg, David Calleo, James Chace, Stephen G. Cohen, Ray Garthoff, Patrick Glyn, Ed Hewett, Walter Isaacson, Bob Kaiser, Walter LaFeber, Michael MccGwire, Don Oberdorfer, and Strobe Talbott, to name only those whose books have been kept closest to hand. To many of those named, I am also grateful for insights gained in discussions and conversation, as well as their work in print. And a great debt is also due to Dr Kenneth Courtis, perhaps the leading Western expert on the Japanese and East Asian economies, for his advice and insights, and to the indispensable Dr Georgi Arbatov of Moscow.

Any merits this book may have stem from the way that I have been able to clamber on to the shoulders of these and other scholars, and use their work to try and see the global experience of the Cold War from a slightly different and sometimes wider point of view. All the errors and misjudgements are, of course, my own.

The greatest debt is due to my family, who put up with my long absences and distractions and encouraged and sustained me throughout. My wife Julia has shared many of the experiences, from Afghanistan to Moscow and Washington, and helped me make sense of them, while our daughters Kate and Fanny embody the life and promise that comes after the Cold War. This book is dedicated to them, in the hope that they will know an even longer and more productive peace.

Martin Walker,
Washington DC

Introduction

Two things of opposite natures seem to depend
On one another, as a man depends
On a woman, day on night, the imagined
On the real. This is the origin of change.

'Two Things', Wallace Stevens

The history of the Cold War has been the history of the world since 1945. Communications and missile technology required the Cold War's proxy battle zones to girdle the entire earth and its satellites to orbit above. The Cold War was truly a global conflict, more so than either of the century's two world wars. South America and sub-Saharan Africa, continents which had been largely spared the earlier struggles, were sucked into its maw. Turks fought in Korea, Algerians fought in Vietnam, Cubans fought in Angola, and American and Russian schoolchildren, whose lessons had been interrupted by nuclear air-raid drills, grew up to die in Saigon and Kabul.

For all its economic and psychological burdens, and despite the appalling consequences in those parts of the developing world where the superpowers fought their wars by proxy, the Cold War had one great merit: it became an institution, marked by a kind of warped stability and an evolving code of acceptable behaviour, which helped spare humanity the devastation of a Third World War. The Cold War was also the first total war between economic and social systems, an industrial test to destruction. Victory became clear when the Soviet economy in the 1980s cracked under the strain of devoting an ever-larger proportion of gross national product (GNP) and research resources in the vain attempt to keep pace. The West prevailed because its economy proved able to supply guns as well as butter, aircraft-carriers *and* private cars, rockets as well as foreign holidays for an ever-increasing proportion of its taxpayers.

The West developed a peculiar mix of free enterprise and state investment, which generated an unprecedented synergy between private prosperity and defence-orientated public spending. The US Inter-state Highway Network was originally funded under a National Security Act, to speed evacuation of the cities under the threat of nuclear attack, and to facilitate the movement of troops. The surge in US college education after the 1950s was equally funded and justified in terms of national security: the need to catch up with a Soviet adversary which had put the first Sputnik into orbit in 1957, and the first man into space four years later.

In the course of the Cold War, the US became what Senator Daniel Patrick Moynihan has dubbed 'the National Security State', with a vast standing army, a global intelligence network, and a military–industrial economic complex whose booming factories helped spur the post-war growth of California and the Southern states, transforming the industrial and political geography of America.[1] When the Cold War began, the population of California was not quite five million, and Presidential candidates usually hailed from the traditional industrial states or the Atlantic seaboard, with their commercial and ethnic links to Europe. When it ended, the population of California was over thirty million, and it provided more than one in ten of US Congressmen elected in 1992. In Richard Nixon and Ronald Reagan, the new economic superstate of the west had already provided two Presidents.

The economic impact of the Cold War also played an incalculable role in the shaping of the modern economic world. The Cold War was the strategic rationale behind the Marshall Plan and the unprecedented US investment in Western Europe's post-war economic recovery. American aid and later US private investment force-fed the German economic miracle. And for four decades, the US garrison of 300,000 men in West Germany pumped dollars into the local economy and acted as a bridge which facilitated Europe's exports to America. It was the returning US servicemen who made the Volkswagen Beetle the first foreign car to make dramatic inroads into the vast American market.

America's Cold War defence budgets also pumped investment into the now booming economies of the Pacific Rim. Japan's economic miracle can be dated with some precision to the effect of the Korean War, when Japan became the main base for the US war effort. Japan was the rest-and-recreation centre for troops on leave, as well as the beneficiary of the constant flow of pay to the permanent US naval, Marine and Air Force garrisons on Japanese bases. Recovering from the devastation of World War Two, Japanese industry geared up to supply the non-lethal requirements of the US forces, the ports and warehousing centres, the medical equipment and maintenance facilities, the watches and radios and souvenirs the troops took home.

In the 1960s, the US war in Vietnam had a much wider impact across Asia. Japanese Hondas and stereos and radios packed the PX stores on the American bases. The hotel boom of Bangkok followed the Thai capital's designation as a main rest-and-recreation centre. Singapore's dockyards, suffering from the withdrawal of Britain's attenuated fleet, found new customers in the US Navy. Hong Kong's reputation as Asia's duty-free shopping centre was consolidated by the US troops.

The old British Empire had a saying, 'Trade follows the Flag', and America's global deployments of the Cold War fulfilled that prescription to a degree which can be traced in the booming Asia and Western Europe of today. Those booms would probably have happened anyway; the Marshall Plan and the long watch on the Rhine, the Korean and Vietnam wars certainly intensified that process. Above all, they accelerated the dramatic expansion of world trade which helped the American and broader Western economies to the prosperity which was the root of their eventual triumph over the enclosed and far less commercial Soviet system.

At the same time, the American garrisons in Europe and Asia brought with them their music, their cigarettes, their cars and films and Coca-Cola. The sudden shock of American popular culture which hit Europe with the GIs of World War Two was deepened and consolidated by the continued global presence of Americans in the Cold War. It was a soft and seductive form of power whose effect was all the more potent for being subliminal; witness the irony of European students demonstrating furiously against the Vietnam War to the rhythms of rock 'n' roll, or the Kremlin inveighing against America's cultural imperialism as Pepsi went on sale alongside the black-market Levi jeans on Moscow street corners. Even Aeroflot's pilots had no choice but to study English, the language of the world's commercial airways.

The deeper changes which the Cold War brought to the Soviet Union were less immediately apparent. Stalin had imposed a national security state of an incomparably more ruthless and intrusive kind, long before the Cold War began. But the climate of confrontation permitted this repressive system and the militarisation of society to assume a life and a political force of its own, almost irrespective of the efforts at thaw and reform by Stalin's successors. Each time the Soviet leaders tried to redirect their economy towards the production of more consumer goods, the demands of the arms race forced them back into the military–industrial bunker. Khrushchev's demobilisation of a million men in 1957 not only won him the sullen enmity of the officer corps, but the attempted reduction in the defence budget had to be reversed to meet the new American challenge of the Polaris submarines and the Minuteman missiles. Kosygin's economic reforms after 1964 were aborted largely because of the General Staff's demands for a Soviet navy and a strategic nuclear parity to redeem the defeat in the Cuban missile crisis.

An awful symbiosis emerged between the main actors of the Cold War, a rhythm of escalation between the Pentagon and the Soviet strategic rocket forces, and a long secret war between the KGB and the CIA which helped make the spy thriller into the distinctive cultural genre of the period. The two sides became locked into the roles of hero and villain in one another's morality play, as two distinct theories of social and political organisation believed they were grappling for nothing less than the inheritance of the planet.

Had anything like this civil war of the human race ever happened before? There are some intriguing historic parallels: the long twilight struggle of the Roman Empire against the barbarism without and social decay within; the still uncompleted Kulturkampf between Christendom and Islam. Indeed, Dean Acheson, the American Secretary of State during the Cold War's most intense years, observed in his memoirs:

> The threat to Western Europe seemed to me singularly like that which Islam had posed centuries before, with its combination of ideological zeal and fighting power. Then it had taken the same combination to meet it: Germanic power in the east, and Frankish in Spain, both energized by a great outburst of military power and social organization in Europe. This time it would need the added power and energy of America, for the drama was now played on a world stage.[2]

The Europeans claim with justice that they are a great civilisation, consistently cultured and uniquely creative. Their peoples developed the newspaper and the novel, the symphony and the opera, the portrait and the oil painting, the factory and the stock exchange, the parliament and the election. The world has paid a stiff price for this European contribution; Europe also invented the concentration camp and the nation state organised for war. The Europeans at their grandest justified their colonial empires as bringing the benefits of civilisation and Christianity to savage shores and dark continents wracked by tribal strife. But in fact, the fractious European tribes have consistently proved to be the most aggressive and warlike, vicious and even genocidal of all the earth's peoples.

The endemic wars of Europe in the past millennium have been of two broad kinds: wars of ideology, about what other men and women are allowed to believe: and wars of succession and the balance of power. The Cold War, for the first time, combined both of these characteristics of the European mode of war. It was about the balance of power, a war of the German succession, and at the same time it was an ideological confrontation. The Cold War was fought about the fate of Europe, and by the two great successor states of the European tradition, the United States and the old Russian autocracy reborn as the Soviet Union through the ideology of Communism. It was thus the last and greatest of Europe's civil wars.

So while the Cold War became a death struggle between economic and social systems, it was also an internecine strife that was located squarely within the Western intellectual tradition. For all the attempts to portray the Soviet Union as a semi-Asian state, as 'the East', the Soviet side mobilised behind the banner of a classically Western ideology which had been drawn up in the British Museum, based on Marx's studies of the industrial revolution in England, and refined in the political stirrings of the new working class of Germany and France. In purely ideological terms, the confrontation of the Cold War was an extreme version of the continuing political debate between conservative and social democratic parties across Europe. It was a fatally exaggerated form of the ongoing choice between organising societies on a collective or on an individual basis, which is part of the common political vocabulary of North America as well as Europe.

The Revolution of 1917 was launched as an attempt to develop a new kind of collectivised society, an idealist and even utopian bid to replace the tsarist autocracy with a new and fairer and more democratic political vision. But it was also an attempt to modernise and indeed to Westernise a largely peasant and backward land. Communism was the West, in all its furious and industrialising energy, a twentieth-century version of that earlier Westernising process which Peter the Great had imposed upon the virtually feudal Russia of the early eighteenth century. It was no historical accident that launched the Bolshevik Revolution in that city of St Petersburg which the enlightened despot had built and named after himself, and which was to be renamed Leningrad after the Bolshevik leader.

The vision of utopia was marred from the beginning by a ruthless civil war between Reds and Whites. British, French, Japanese, Czech and American troops spasmodically intervened against the Bolsheviks. And the Bolsheviks responded with the deliberate policy of state terror, to secure their grip. Launched by Felix Dzherzhinsky's Cheka, the reliance upon the secret police was to become characteristic of a regime which had begun with fine intentions. But the terror only developed into a characteristic and encompassing feature of the Soviet state under Stalin, and it assumed its full horror after Hitler's Nazi Party came to power in Germany in 1933. The Great Purges were justified in the name of national security as the totalitarian twins of Germany and Russia spent the pre-war years in a curious rehearsal of the Cold War. Stalin's party rivals and the Red Army generals were tried and condemned as German spies. The two systems fought by proxy in the Spanish Civil War, and enjoyed their own calculated phase of *détente* to devour Poland and the Baltic states before Hitler's catastrophic plunge into war in 1941.

It is never easy to argue with success, and the Soviet victory over Nazism not only established Stalin squarely in the heart of central Europe, it also established the grim methods of Stalinism as a tried and tested system which his successors found it difficult to change. Stalin's ruthlessness had industrialised the country, won the war, established a defensive glacis which guaranteed that the German threat would not revive, and crushed domestic dissent. The spasmodic attempts at internal reform and international *détente* by Stalin's heirs always laboured under this dreadful inheritance. The industrial and defence and security establishments which Stalin had built into the very structure of the state were not only durable at home, they also fuelled a constant suspicion and military response in the West. With hindsight, the eventual collapse of the Soviet system may appear to have been inevitable, a deliberate control and suppression of human creativity which was doomed to enfeeble the state's economic and eventually military potential. It did not always seem that way.

Whittaker Chambers, the former Communist agent in the United States who became the main witness against Alger Hiss in the US House of Representatives Committee on Un-American Activities, said that in changing his allegiance, he felt he had joined the losing side.[3] When Khrushchev said, 'We shall bury you', many in the West took it literally.[4] When Communists seized power in China, and when the first Sputnik seemed to herald a Soviet technological lead in 1957, the West tasted the prospect of eventual defeat. And after America's strategic reverse in Vietnam was followed by widespread opposition in Western Europe to deploying new Cruise and Pershing missiles, the most likely outcome of the Cold War seemed to be a kind of stable draw, an endless and uneasy peace of grudging coexistence.

The militarised vocabulary of the Cold War leads us too easily to talk of the West's victory and the Soviet defeat. In reality, the end of the Cold War was just as much a Soviet decision to redirect their frustrated energies to a new challenge, a decisive and still unresolved confrontation with their own internal problems and structures. In legal terms, the Soviets did not plead guilty, but *noli contendere*. In human terms, everyone won, and it was the Cold War itself which lost. It had endured long enough to become more than simply a way of life, rather a structure and defining context within which world events took their warped shape. Americans, Russians, Europeans and eventually the rest of the world became its prisoners, hostages to the nuclear balance which the world's leading economies strained themselves to maintain.

But at the same time, the Cold War became a form of global insurance against catastrophe, a system of political control which prevented local wars from getting out of hand. A stabilising paradox emerged in which smaller nations pursued their own policies and conflicts in the shadow of the superpowers, but the price of US or Soviet support and arms supplies was a surrender of an important aspect of their sovereignty to the strategic priorities of Moscow and Washington. The superpowers did not permit, because they dared not risk, a regional conflict developing into a total war. That constraint is now being removed, just at a time when smaller powers from India to Israel have developed their own nuclear capacity, and the missile technology to deliver the warheads which were once the monopoly of the superpower condominium. The defeated Soviet Empire has crumbled into the component parts which tsarism assembled and which Stalin welded into a gruesome homomorph, half Gulag and half tank. The familiar dangers of the Cold War have ended; the unknown perils of its aftermath lie in wait.

Chapter 1

1945: Yalta to the Bomb

Yes, Russia is a Sphinx. Exulting, grieving
And sweating blood, she cannot sate
Her eyes that gaze and gaze and gaze
At stone-lipped love for you, and hate.
Get you all gone to Ural fastnesses.
We clear the ground for the appalling scenes
Of war between the savage Mongol hordes
And pitiless science with its massed machines.

'The Scythians', Alexander

On 4 February 1945, with victory in sight and their armies poised to invade the German heartland, the leaders of the Grand Alliance met at the ancient Black Sea resort of the Tsars to agree the design for the post-war world. The site was carefully chosen. In a Soviet Union ravaged and exhausted by the German invasion, the old Livadia summer palace was a rare and relatively unspoilt sanctuary. Built for Tsar Nicholas in 1913, Livadia was the centre of a complex of palaces along the lovely Crimean shore, where the Soviet leaders could assert and display their inheritance of an older Russian empire.

Stalin himself took over the Koreis palace of Prince Yusupov. Winston Churchill and his British delegation were housed in the Vorontsov palace, some twelve miles away. Its stately park was dotted with 'stone wives', statues of women that had been recovered by archaeologists from the graves of the twelfth-century warriors of the steppes. Living women were also a feature of Soviet hospitality. Field Marshal Lord Alexander recalled having to ask 'a sort of female valet, dressed in a kind of nurse's uniform' to sleep outside his room, where she had evidently intended to spend the night.[1] Rank has its privileges. The American delegation was housed in the Livadia palace itself, in conditions of such crowding that sixteen colonels had to share a single room with the bedbugs.[2]

The Yalta conference was hailed at the time as a new and hopeful departure in human events. At the final caviare dinner hosted by Stalin on 8 February, in a toast to Churchill and Stalin, President Roosevelt said he felt the atmosphere between them 'was that of a family'. Stalin said he was convinced that 'our relations in peacetime should be as strong as they had been in war'. Ever the orator, Winston Churchill replied that he 'felt we are all standing on the crest of a hill with the glories of future possibilities before us'. For Harry Hopkins, Roosevelt's closest adviser and his special envoy to other heads of state, 'We really believed in our hearts that this was the dawn of the new day we had all been praying for.'[3]

It was a grim day for the German city of Dresden. At a meeting on the first day of the Yalta conference with the British and American chiefs of staff, the Soviet deputy chief of staff General Antonov asked for air support to stop German reinforcements being moved to the Soviet front. He asked in particular for the transport centres of Berlin, Leipzig and Dresden to be 'allotted to the Allied air forces'. From the night of 13 February until the morning of 15 February, waves of some twelve hundred British and US bombers devastated Dresden. When it ended, 39,773 people were officially registered as dead. Another 20,000 are believed to have been burnt beyond recognition as corpses. 'Who knows the number?' says the inscription at Dresden cemetery.[4]

The destruction of Dresden is the clearest reminder that when the Big Three met at Yalta, the most destructive war of history was still being fought. By 1945, fifty countries had joined the Allied cause, including Guatemala and Liberia, and mobilised sixty million people into their armies. At least ten million of them died, although the figures for China and the Soviet Union remain vague. A comparison of the pre-war against the post-war Soviet census suggests that the combined civilian and military death toll was close to twenty-five million, but that would include the monstrous toll of Stalin's Gulag. Nine countries, including Albania and Thailand, had joined the cause of the Axis and mobilised some thirty million troops, and at least six million of them died. The civilian casualties, from starvation and disease and bombing and death camp, were higher than the military, as half the globe was sucked into the maw of a vast, industrialised war machine, whose American factories alone spewed out 296,000 warplanes, 86,000 tanks and 11,900 ships.[5]

So Yalta's diplomatic negotiations and the dispositions of the post-war world were made amid the brutal urgencies of military decisions designed to bring about the agreed war aim of Germany's unconditional surrender. And it was that very war aim which contained the roots of the Cold War. Unconditional surrender, when Hitler was able to keep his armies fighting to the last bunker in Berlin, meant the destruction of everything which made up the German state. Germany's armed forces, its system of internal government and communications, its economy and its food and distribution systems, were all to be devastated by the final surrender in May 1945. By the end of the war, Germany was a humanitarian disaster and a political and military vacuum which the victorious Allies had to feed and fill.

They were ill-equipped to do so. They had another war to fight and win, against Japan in the Pacific. The three allies also faced the end of the war in Europe with different, and potentially incompatible, strategic objectives. Stalin wanted security, a Germany that could never threaten to invade Russia again, as it had done twice in the past thirty years, and a wide defensive belt of friendly territory in Eastern Europe, just in case. 'Friendly', in this context, meant ready to subordinate their national sovereignty to Soviet interests. In practice, this meant client states with Soviet-style governments, protected by a secret police and with a state-controlled economic system that would not allow the emergence of a prosperous middle class. Such property-owners, said Karl Marx's orthodoxy and Stalin's suspicions, would inevitably seek an independent political role to match their economic weight.

Stalin's entirely rational objectives threatened the policy Britain had adopted in Europe since the days of the Kaiser, of Napoleon, of the Sun King Louis XIV and even of the Spanish Armada in the sixteenth century: to ensure that no single power dominated the European continent, as Stalin now threatened to do. The Americans wanted peace and trade, an amicable and democratic new order in Europe. But they also wanted to bring their troops home from Europe as fast as possible, partly because of the immediate priority of the war against Japan, and partly because Congress was impatient. 'Two years would be the limit,' Roosevelt told a silently watchful Stalin, and an appalled Churchill.[6] 'If the Americans left Europe, Britain would have to occupy single-handed the entire Western portion of Germany. Such a task would be far beyond our strength,' Churchill noted privately.[7] The crushing of Germany created an opportunity which only Stalin seemed able to seize.

At that moment, the hitherto barely foreseen results of the war crystallised. Nominally a victor of the Grand Alliance, Britain's victory was Pyrrhic, bought at a price so high that its role as a Great Power could no longer be sustained. This meant that the cardinal principle of British policy thereafter would be to maintain an American military presence in Europe. The alternative would be Soviet domination of a hollow continent in which Britain was too weak to play its traditional role of the balancing power.

This was the nightmare that Churchill had dreaded in the early summer of 1944, when the Soviet armies were racing into Poland and the Balkans. 'The Russians are drunk with victory and there is no length to which they may not go,' he had written to his foreign secretary, Anthony Eden.[8] To forestall too sweeping a Russian occupation, the British pressed – not for the last time – for a swift invasion of Germany in the hope of reaching Berlin before the Soviet armies. In September 1944, British and American airborne forces were parachuted across the Rhine at Arnhem in one of the boldest failures of the war. Churchill flew to Moscow the following month, in the hope that the traditional diplomacy of realism could secure what the paratroopers had failed to win.

At 10 pm on 9 October, Churchill met Stalin in the Kremlin and said, 'How would it do for you to have ninety per cent predominance in Rumania, for us to have ninety per cent of the say in Greece, and go fifty-fifty about Yugoslavia?' Churchill sketched out the figures on a sheet of paper, adding 50–50 for Hungary, and 75–25 in Bulgaria (in Stalin's favour). Stalin 'took his blue pencil and made a large tick upon it, and passed it back to us'.[9] The British Foreign Office memorandum of the conversation also records that Stalin accepted that Britain after the war would be 'the leading Mediterranean power'.[10] The famous sheet of paper contained no reference to Germany or Czechoslovakia, nor to Poland, the country for which Britain had gone to war in 1939, but which had become in Churchill's eyes a hopeless cause. Just before he left for Yalta, Churchill confided to his personal secretary: 'Make no mistake, all the Balkans, except Greece, are going to be Bolshevised, and there is nothing I can do to prevent it. There is nothing I can do for Poland either.'[11]

The promise of Allied victory in 1944 led to almost a year of mutual suspicion, which the Yalta conference was intended to resolve. Stalin suspected that Britain and America were plotting a separate peace with Germany, precisely in order to fend off Soviet domination of central Europe.[12] Stalin's motives in halting his armies on the outskirts to Warsaw, to watch the rising of the Polish Home Army crushed by German troops, aroused British and American contempt, mixed with the belief that Stalin wanted the German slaughter to create a political vacuum in Poland that could be filled by his Communist clients. Western diplomats begged for landing and refuelling rights at

Soviet-held airfields, to allow its aircraft in Italy to supply the besieged Polish resistance. Until it was too late, Stalin refused. 'It was the toughest talk I ever had with a Soviet official,' US Ambassador Averell Harriman recalled.[13]

Warsaw's agony in 1944 threw into question the fate of liberated Europe after the war. In public, there were protestations of Allied solidarity. In private, Churchill's fears of Soviet ambition were becoming widespread among American officials too. 'There was no time when the danger from the Soviet Union was not a topic of anxious conversation among officers of the State Department,' recalled Louis Halle, of the Policy Planning Staff. 'And by the winter of 1944–5, as the day of victory approached, it became the predominant theme in Washington.'[14] It was also the main concern of American diplomats and military attachés in Moscow, whose direct experience of the Kremlin made them markedly more suspicious of Soviet intentions than their political masters back home. In September, Ambassador Harriman wrote to the White House: 'Unless we take issue with the present policy, there is every indication the Soviet Union will become a world bully.'[15] Harriman's chief adviser, George Kennan, later to be celebrated as the father of the policy of containment, set down in that autumn of 1944 what was to become the basic principle of Western policy towards the Soviets for a generation. Kennan stressed the need 'to determine in conjunction with the British the line beyond which we cannot afford to permit the Russians to exercise unchallenged power'.[16]

For Churchill, and for his generals, and for an influential group of American officials if not for President Roosevelt, the battle lines of the future were already being drafted before Yalta, as the simple geography of Soviet military occupation defined a new political reality in Europe. Stalin evidently agreed, telling the 1944 military mission from Yugoslavia that: 'This war is not as in the past; whoever occupies a territory also imposes on it his own social system. Everyone imposes his own system as far as his army has power to do so. It cannot be otherwise.'[17] Roosevelt and his high command differed. On the eve of the Yalta conference, the US and British chiefs of staff met in Malta to plan the next phase of the attack on Germany. This provoked one of the most bitter Allied disputes of the war. The British urged again a swift armoured spearhead to occupy Berlin, while from Italy another assault should seek to take Vienna and Prague before the Red Army could create tomorrow's political facts on today's battlefields. The Americans point-blank refused, insisting that they would not take casualties for political reasons. General George C. Marshall, the army chief of staff, said that if the British plan were adopted, he would recommend to the supreme allied commander in Europe, General Eisenhower, that he had 'no choice but to ask to be relieved of his command'.[18]

So the Yalta gathering opened with each of the Big Three at odds with the other, in an atmosphere of suspicion, and facing the divisive issue of the kind of European future their victory over Germany would produce. The intimacy of Anglo-American relations, during the war against Germany and later in the long confrontation against the Soviet Union, was by no means guaranteed as the Big Three met at Yalta. It was no part of Roosevelt's war aims to restore the pre-war British Empire, and he told Stalin privately at Yalta that he thought Hong Kong should be returned to the Chinese, or internationalised as a free port.[19]

The last of the wartime conferences, Yalta was also the first of the post-war summits, and this duality of character helps explain Yalta's subsequent grim reputation. Immediately hailed around the world as a landmark in human history, and read aloud to cheers in the US Senate, the communiqué of the Yalta summit gave little hint of the furious denunciations it would later attract. The main tasks of the conference were to agree on plans to end the war in Europe, to win the war against Japan in Asia, and then to settle the broad outlines of the peace. There was much give and take. Stalin agreed to Britain's insistence that the French also be allowed an occupation zone in Germany, after Churchill said that without French power, Britain did not feel able to contain the western front of Germany alone.[20] Difficult issues, like the amount of German reparations, and the number of votes the Soviet Union would have at the future United Nations, were put off to the new structure of regular meetings of foreign ministers.

For the British and Americans, the immediate object was to secure a firm promise and a date for Soviet military support for the final phase of defeating Japan. The plans of General Douglas MacArthur assumed Soviet support to hold down the Japanese armies on the mainland, while British and American forces invaded Japan's home islands. The Soviet pledge to join the war in the Far East was secured when an overnight note from President Roosevelt to Stalin, hurriedly translated over breakfast by Andrei Gromyko, promised to grant Stalin his booty of the Kurile Islands and Sakhalin.[21] This was a classic example of horse-trading between Great Powers, sitting oddly with the grand principles of high-minded international behaviour which Woodrow Wilson had made characteristic of American diplomacy.

There was much high-mindedness at Yalta, but the most ruthless *realpolitik* was deployed to ensure that the Red Army would spill some of the blood required in the final defeat of Japan. The idealism was reserved for the agreement to establish the United Nations, and in the document on the future of the liberated territories which was to be at the heart of the subsequent debate about the blame for the Cold War.

Since this is the text upon which all future accusations of Soviet betrayal and bad faith were made, it is worth quoting at length. The Americans pressed for this Declaration because of political pressure at home, focused above all on the fate of Poland, and backed up by the votes of some seven million Polish-Americans. The Declaration on Liberated Europe started by repeating the principles of the Atlantic Charter: 'The right of all peoples to choose the form of government under which they will live, the restoration of sovereign rights and self-government to those peoples who have been forcibly deprived of them by the aggressor nations.' The crucial paragraph went on:[22]

> To foster the conditions in which the liberated peoples may exercise these rights, the three governments will jointly assist the people in any European liberated state or former Axis satellite state in Europe where in their judgment conditions require: (a) to establish conditions of internal peace; (b) to carry out emergency measures for the relief of distressed peoples; (c) to form interim governmental authorities broadly representative of all democratic elements in the population and pledged to the earliest possible establishment through free elections of governments responsive to the will of the people; and (d) to facilitate where necessary the holding of such elections.

This read well, and Roosevelt was much relieved by this apparent Soviet concession, but the wording was essentially meaningless. 'Democratic elements' meant one thing to Stalin, and quite another to Winston Churchill, who observed wryly at Yalta that he was the only one of the Big Three who could be ejected from office at any time by the votes of his own people.[23] Churchill was right: unless death intervened, an American President had a tenure of four years. 'Free elections' and 'the will of the people' were elastic phrases. This was a document designed to paper over differences, after Stalin had made the point brutally clear. 'Mr Churchill had said that for Great Britain the Polish question was one of honour and that he understood, but for the Russians it was a question both of honour and security,' Stalin said, according to the American transcript. 'Throughout history,

Poland had been the corridor for attack on Russia . . . It was not only a question of honour for Russia, but one of life and death.'[24]

Behind Stalin's words lay the reality of the war still raging, and of centuries of Russian history. Through Poland had come Hitler's tanks, and a generation before that, Kaiser Wilhelm's armies had taken the same route to the Peace of Brest-Litovsk which had wrenched the Baltic states and the Ukraine from the beleaguered Bolsheviks. A century earlier, Napoleon had followed the Polish route to take and burn Moscow in 1812. The century before that, it had been the turn of the Swedes, and the century before them, the Poles had occupied the Kremlin. Russia, a country without natural boundaries like France's River Rhine, or Britain's twenty-one miles of Channel, or America's wide ocean moats, had been invaded by each of its neighbours.

Stalin's obsessive fear of attack was obvious to Churchill, who had supported the British invasion of Lenin's Russia in 1919, arguing the need 'to throttle the infant Bolshevism in its cradle'. American troops had joined that abortive massed attack by the capitalist world upon the young Communist state, along with French, Polish, Czech and Japanese forces. This evidence of history led Stalin to insist on keeping the Red Army's territorial gains as a matter of national security, whatever the Western powers might say, and so did the Communist ideology he still professed. As Lenin had put it, in words which Western anti-Communists seldom tired of reciting: 'As long as capitalism and socialism exist, we cannot live in peace; in the end, one or the other will triumph. A funeral dirge will be sung either over the Soviet Republic or over Capitalism.'[25]

Churchill had few illusions about the fate of Poland, or the form of Europe that would follow the Yalta summit. Roosevelt had many, and expressed them to an enthusiastic joint session of Congress on his return to Washington on 2 March. Roosevelt's optimism helped deepen America's subsequent disillusion, as Stalin's definition of an independent, democratic Poland turned out to be very different from that Roosevelt hoped he had achieved. 'The Crimean Conference ought to spell the end of the system of unilateral action, the exclusive alliance, the spheres of influence, the balance of power, and all the other expedients that have been tried for centuries, and have always failed,' Roosevelt told Congress, in terms which echoed Woodrow Wilson's pious hopes of a seemly new international etiquette after the First World War.[26] The first critique came within a month, in *Time* magazine, in the form of a viciously elegant fantasy. It was written by

Whittaker Chambers, the former Communist agent turned conservative who would later be chief accuser for the crusades of Congressman Richard Nixon and Senator Joe McCarthy against Soviet agents in the US government. Called 'Ghosts on the Roof', the essay imagined the spirits of the last Tsar, Nicholas II, and his wife, sitting on the roof of the Livadia palace and eavesdropping on the negotiations. His admiration for Stalin mounting as the Soviet leader secured strategic advantages and conquests for Russia that the tsarist empire had never achieved, the Tsar declared that he too will become a Communist.[27]

Chambers had a point. By the end of the European war, Soviet dominance of Eastern and central Europe was a military fact, embracing a political reach of which the Tsars had only dreamed. The Red Armies had advanced to a hundred miles west of Berlin, had occupied the eastern halves of Austria and Czechoslovakia, including Vienna and Prague, and dominated the Balkans. The Yalta conference had promised to give Russian warships easier access to the Mediterranean through the Dardanelles, a strategic goal the Tsars had never reached, and also recovered the position in the Far East that tsarist Russia had lost after their humiliating defeat by Japan in 1905. It was a vast extension of the Soviet empire to be held down, and all that the world had learned about the means of Soviet domestic control in the 1930s suggested that their regime would not be pretty. Even before Yalta, Harriman warned from Moscow of 'the institution of secret police who may become involved in the persecution of persons of truly democratic convictions who may not be willing to conform to Soviet methods'. And as Roosevelt was addressing Congress, the State Department was reading the cables from Bucharest, describing how Andrei Vyshinsky, the Soviet deputy commissar for foreign affairs, interpreted the spirit of Yalta. Visiting the Romanian capital, Vyshinsky stormed into the King's study, slammed his fist on the table and demanded a new, pro-Moscow government. When the King of Romania demurred, noting that the Yalta agreement guaranteed free elections, Vyshinsky looked at his watch. 'I will announce the new government in exactly two hours and five minutes,' Vyshinsky snapped, and stalked out, slamming the door so hard the plaster cracked.[28]

The immediate victims of Yalta were the Soviet prisoners of war, many of them Ukrainians or Balts or other unwilling members of Stalin's empire, who had been persuaded to take up arms on Hitler's behalf against the Red Army. But they were not the only prisoners transferred to Stalin's grim mercies by the US and British forces. Civilians and ordinary POWs, Jews from the concentration camps

and an unknown fraction of the displaced persons who wandered the
devastation of post-war Europe, were caught in the implacable net.
The loathsome business of forcing them back into Stalin's arms at
gunpoint provoked suicides among the hapless prisoners, and near-
mutinies among the appalled British troops. But with British and
American POWs still inside the Soviet zone, and British and American
lives to be saved by securing Soviet support for the last campaign
against Japan, the orders and priorities from London were clear.[29]

The next victims of Yalta were American illusions. Within days it
became clear that Stalin's promise of democracy and independence in
Poland did not include any serious political role for the Polish
government-in-exile which had spent the war in London. 'We began
to realize that Stalin's language was somewhat different from ours:
"Friendly neighbours" had an entirely different connotation to him,'
Harriman recalled. 'I am outraged,' he cabled back to the White
House in March, when the Russians refused to let American medical
teams into Poland to treat and evacuate American prisoners of war.
On 3 April, Harriman reported that the Polish talks had degenerated
to breaking point, and asked to come home. Harriman planned to
take with him an eight-page memorandum drafted on 21 March,
which could not have been more bluntly phrased: 'Unless we wish to
accept the 20th century barbarian invasion of Europe, with repercus-
sions extending further and further in the East as well, we must find
ways to arrest the Soviet domineering policy . . . If we don't face these
issues squarely now, history will record the period of the next
generation as the Soviet age.'[30]

In the final days of his life, Roosevelt seemed to agree. At Warm
Springs, receiving one of Harriman's angry telegrams after lunch,
Anna Hoffman reported that the dying President slammed his fists on
his wheelchair and declared, 'Averell is right. We can't do business
with Stalin.'[31] But Roosevelt's last reply to the Moscow Embassy on
12 April called for more conciliation, and he died that day. His policy,
however, of refusing finally to believe the worst of his Soviet comrade-
in-arms would outlive him for some time.

The new President Harry Truman came into office with little
preparation for foreign affairs, and his one striking comment on
relations with the Soviet Union had been made in the week Hitler
invaded in 1941: 'If we see that Germany is winning we ought to help
Russia, and if Russia is winning we ought to help Germany, and that
way let them kill as many as possible although I don't want to see
Hitler victorious under any circumstances.'[32]

Truman's education in Soviet policy was to be equally blunt. On his second day as President, Truman was given a report on the international situation by Secretary of State Edward Stettinius, which warned him: 'Since the Yalta conference the Soviet government has taken a firm and uncompromising position on nearly every major question.'[33] He was also delivered a solemn report drafted for Roosevelt on 2 April by the wartime intelligence agency, the Office of Strategic Services. The first warning that the future security of the United States was at stake, as well as the fate of Poland, it said: 'Russia will emerge from the present conflict as by far the strongest nation in Europe and Asia, strong enough, if the United States should stand aside, to dominate Europe and at the same time to establish her hegemony over Asia . . . In the easily foreseeable future Russia may well outrank even the US in military potential.'[34]

The warnings could hardly have been clearer. But Harriman was to make them even harsher, returning from Moscow to press his views on the new President. He began by convincing the President's top advisers. Over dinner with Navy Secretary Forrestal on 19 April, Harriman stressed that 'the outward thrust of Communism was not dead, and that we well might have to face an ideological warfare just as vigorous and dangerous as Fascism or Nazism'. The next day he gave a special seminar for the senior officials at the State Department, to warn: 'The Soviet Union, once it had control of bordering areas, would attempt to penetrate the next adjacent countries . . . This issue ought to be fought out insofar as we can with the Soviet Union in the present bordering areas.'[35]

From that meeting in the State Department building just west of the White House, Harriman strolled across to see the new President. With him came the Secretary of State Stettinius, the veteran Moscow diplomat Chip Bohlen, and Under-Secretary Joseph Grew. But it was Harriman, fresh from Moscow, embodying not only the vast wealth from the family railroad fortune but the mantle of Roosevelt's wartime alliance with Stalin, who dominated the meeting. It was a crucial moment, the chance for Harriman to convince the innocent new President that the pledges given to Roosevelt at Yalta were being broken. He began with that dark phrase he had crafted in Moscow – 'the barbarian invasion of Europe'. But Harriman knew that what Truman needed was not just warnings, but practical policy advice. A new and more realistic basis was needed for working with the Russians, a tough policy that made it clear there were benefits available for cooperation, and penalties for hostility.

Truman, a veteran of the horse-trading way of Senate politics, seized at once upon the thought of bargains. He could not expect to get one hundred per cent from the Russians, he said, but on the big issues he expected to get eighty-five per cent, and Poland would have to be resolved under the principles agreed at Yalta. 'I intend to tell Molotov that in words of one syllable.'[36]

On 23 April, Truman convened a long and crucial briefing in the White House by his Russian experts. This was the moment when the balance in American policy began to shift, away from Roosevelt's wartime trust, to Truman's post-war suspicion. The briefing took place immediately before Truman's meeting with Soviet foreign minister Vyacheslav Molotov, who was on his way to San Francisco for the first UN meetings. Stalin had only agreed to send Molotov as a gesture to Roosevelt's memory, and it was to be Truman's first confrontation with the Soviet leadership. The preliminary meeting of the Americans was attended by the men who had run the war from Washington, Roosevelt's intimates, and Truman was still, if not awed, then deeply respectful of their collective wisdom. He was surrounded by Roosevelt's war cabinet: Colonel Henry Stimson, the Secretary for War; General Marshall; Admiral Leahy; Secretary of State Stettinius; Navy Secretary Forrestal; with Harriman and the US military attaché to Moscow, General John Deane.

The meeting was the more important because, just ten weeks after Yalta, Roosevelt's old war cabinet no longer shared a consensus. Stettinius began by reporting the previous evening's meeting at the State Department with Molotov and the British foreign secretary, Sir Anthony Eden. 'Great difficulties had developed over the Polish question,' and they had continued at a further meeting that morning, Stettinius went on. It was now clear that the Russians were trying to force their own puppet government upon Britain and the United States. President Truman, saying that relations with Moscow had so far been 'a one-way street', asked the rest of his advisers for their views.

The Russians had always kept their word 'in the big military matters', said Stimson. The real veteran of the cabinet, Stimson warned against 'a collision', and voiced his 'fear we are rushing into a situation where we would find ourselves breaking our relations with Russia'. Forrestal disagreed, warning that Poland was not the only breach of Yalta; Bulgaria and Romania were going the same way. Harriman said the issue was plain, whether 'the US should be a party to Soviet domination of Poland'. Properly and firmly handled, Harriman went on, this need not lead to a break with Russia. Admiral

Leahy spoke of the agreements made at Yalta, and said he was sure the Russians would never permit free elections in Poland. Stettinius then read aloud the Yalta declaration which Stalin had signed.

General Marshall said he leaned to Stimson's view, for the military reasons which had weighed so heavily at Yalta. A breach with Russia could delay their entry into the war against Japan 'until we have done all the dirty work'. Truman returned to what he saw as the core of the issue – 'the execution of agreements entered into between this government and the Soviet Union'. Seeing the meeting was swinging his way, Harriman spoke up again. He agreed with Stimson that the military agreements which Russia had kept were 'decisions it had already made for itself, but on other military matters it was impossible to say they had lived up to their commitments'. Harriman was then followed by his ally from the Moscow Embassy, General Deane, who spoke of his own experience in the Soviet capital, and advised, 'if we were afraid of the Russians we would get nowhere; we should be firm when we were right'. Truman, just twelve days into office, said cautiously that he would follow the views of the majority.[37]

The hard-line views which Harriman brought with him from Moscow had won. The new policy had begun, and later that day, it was slammed on to the table before the Russians for the first time. Molotov entered the Oval Office, accompanied by Ambassador Gromyko, to be told bluntly by Truman of his 'deep disappointment' that the Yalta agreement on Poland was not being met. Citing opinion in Congress and American public opinion, Truman then gave him a message for immediate delivery to Stalin, which warned that the failure to fulfil the Yalta agreement 'would seriously shake confidence in the unity of the three governments'. As Molotov went into a long reply, Truman intervened four times, each time more sharply, stressing 'there was only one thing to do, and that was for Marshal Stalin to carry out that agreement in accordance with his word'.

'I have never been talked to like that in my life,' protested Molotov.

'Carry out your agreements, and you won't get talked to like that,' snapped Truman. And in Gromyko's account: 'Quite unexpectedly, still in the middle of our talk, Truman suddenly half rose and gave a sign to indicate that our conversation was over, in effect breaking off the meeting.' In retrospect, Gromyko thought, Truman's 'stridently pugnacious' attitude could be explained only by the knowledge that the United States now had the atom bomb. In fact, it was two days later that Colonel Stimson first briefed the new President of 'the most terrible weapon ever known in human history, one bomb of which could destroy a whole city'.[38]

Through Soviet eyes, the new American stance was alarming and suspicious. Stalin's fears deepened three weeks later, when Truman celebrated the German surrender on 5 May by shutting off the Lend-Lease shipments to Britain and to Russia, so brusquely that some ships turned around in mid-ocean. After howls of outrage from London and Moscow, Truman softened the policy. But when his personal envoy Harry Hopkins met Stalin in Moscow on 27 May, Stalin growled that if this was 'designed as pressure on the Russians in order to soften them up it was a serious mistake'. Stalin went on to complain that the US–British decision to allow France to join the post-war Reparations Commission was 'an insult', since France had 'opened the frontier to the Germans'. And on Poland, Stalin cited the text of Yalta as implying that the other Allies had agreed that the pro-Soviet provisional government should be the basis for the new regime: 'No other understanding of the Yalta agreement was possible. Despite the fact that the Russians were a simple people, they should not be regarded as fools, which was a mistake the West frequently made.'[39]

Worse was to come. When Harriman had suggested to Truman that the policy of firmness could be backed up by the carrot of American economic aid in return for cooperation, he had in mind the Soviet application for American credits of $6 billion* for post-war reconstruction. The request had been made by Molotov in January 1945 and put off for later by the Americans. It had been mentioned again at Yalta, and again without an American response. As if embarrassed by the American silence, the Soviets did not raise the matter again until August, when their troops were already fulfilling the Yalta agreement by fighting the Japanese in Manchuria, and were told to Moscow's disbelief that the Americans could find no trace of their financial request. In fact, it seems to have been lost when the records of the Foreign Economic Administration were transferred to the State Department. Accident it may have been; after the rows over Poland, it did not look that way to the Russians.[40]

Stalin might have been relieved to learn that the British, too, felt that they were suddenly being treated shabbily by their American ally. The British were equally worried by the interruption of Lend-Lease in May, and their fears were confirmed when Truman cancelled the programme altogether just eight days after the Japanese surrender in August. Bankrupt after sustaining over two years of war alone, and being forced to sell all British holdings in America, Britain had

---

* In this book, 'billion' is used to mean '1,000 million' and 'trillion' to mean '1,000,000 million'.

assigned its leading economist, John Maynard Keynes, to handle the delicate financial negotiations. He initially faced an American Treasury Secretary, Henry Morgenthau, whose policies were to reduce Germany to an agrarian economy, and 'to move the financial centre of the world from London and Wall Street to the US Treasury'.[41] Morgenthau was removed in Truman's first cabinet reshuffle in July 1945, possibly because he had favoured 'a concrete plan to aid them [the Russians] in their reconstruction period'.[42]

Even with the advocacy of the formidable Keynes, who brought personal experience of the 1919 Treaty of Versailles to the post-war financial talks, the British were appalled by the American positions. There was a mood of something close to betrayal, that the loyal British ally was being plundered while she was down, among both Churchill's government and the Labour government under Clement Attlee which replaced it after the general election in July.

The US had supplied its British ally some $27 billion in Lend-Lease items of food and munitions, and Britain had sent the US some $6 billion in reverse Lend-Lease goods. Under the final deal, Britain had to pay another $650 million in cash to settle the account. To pay that, and to pay for food imports while its economy was still mobilised for war, Britain needed a loan of $3.75 billion. This was agreed, at what Britain felt was an unfriendly 2 per cent interest rate over fifty years. Worse still, this followed the Bretton Woods conference on the future global economy which established the dollar as the world's main reserve currency, freely convertible into gold, pushing the pound sterling into second place. This was not only a blow to British pride, it also burdened the pound with an international trading responsibility which it simply could not sustain without American economic support. To get the American loan, the British were forced to agree to ratify the Bretton Woods deal in full, and to make sterling freely exchangeable against the dollar within a year. In practice, this meant that the British were forced to open up their protected colonial markets, their main hope of export growth and long-term recovery, to American competition. This was done as a deliberate act of US policy, in sharp contrast to the later generosity of the Marshall Plan. 'We loaded the British loan negotiations with all the traffic the market could bear,' reported Will Clayton, the American negotiator.[43]

The political effect of these technical economic arrangements upon Anglo-American relations was appalling. Before the year was out, it was dubbed in Parliament 'an economic Munich', and the Americans were accused of using their economic muscle to take over Britain's protected markets in the colonies. 'Selling the British Empire for a packet of cigarettes,' sneered Tory MP Robert Boothby, noting that such terms of settlement were usually reserved for defeated enemies. Even *The Economist*, a traditionally pro-American weekly, noted: 'It is aggravating to find that the reward for losing a quarter of our national wealth in the common cause is to pay tribute for half a century to those who have been enriched by the war.'[44]

At the same time, Truman simply repealed the joint authority for nuclear weapons which Roosevelt had agreed with Churchill when British scientists were first assigned to the Anglo-American-Canadian Manhattan Project. Again, the Americans claimed to have lost their copy of the accord the two men had signed on 19 September 1944, which said 'full collaboration . . . for military and commercial purposes should continue after the defeat of Japan'.[45] In June, Churchill sent a photograph of his own copy, but it did little good. Under Congressional pressure, Truman signed the McMahon Act into law the following year. This effectively barred the United States from sharing atomic secrets with anyone, even the British who had begun the research.

Nor was Truman eager to tell the Soviets about it. On 16 July, the eve of the Potsdam summit, the news was flashed to Truman that the first atom-bomb test in New Mexico had proved successful. Further news had to wait another five days, for the first detailed report reached Berlin by courier. It took Stimson an hour to read aloud to his President the news that the bomb had 'far exceeded most optimistic expectations and wildest hopes of the scientists'. Truman, Stimson recalled, was 'tremendously pepped up',[46] so much so that a baffled Churchill later asked whatever had come over the President. Only the next day did Churchill understand, when Stimson read to him the report from New Mexico. Three days after that, on 24 July, Truman 'casually mentioned to Stalin that we had a new weapon of unusually destructive force'.[47]

What Truman did not say to Stalin was that earlier in the day he and Churchill and their chiefs of staff had sat around a table in the gloomy dining-room of No. 2, Kaiserstrasse, and agreed to drop it on Japan by 10 August. Gunpowder and electricity were meaningless by comparison, Churchill had observed. 'The atomic bomb is the Second Coming – in Wrath.' The first had been bad enough, the evidence of the power of conventional bombing in the devastation of Berlin all around them. It had stunned Truman, who scribbled almost random names of ruin and war's horror into his diary after his first sight of Berlin: 'I thought of Carthage, Baalbek, Jerusalem, Rome, Atlantis, Peking . . . of Scipio, Rameses II, Sherman, Jenghiz Khan.' What none of the men sitting around that table in Kaiserstrasse could have known was that the room in which the atomic decision was first taken had only weeks before been witness to an older horror; ten weeks of gang rape by Soviet troops upon the daughters of the German publisher Gustav Müller-Grote. It had been his house, and he and his grandchildren had been beaten and made to watch, until the family had been evicted to make way for what Truman called his 'Little White House'.[48]

As Truman, Stalin and Churchill met at Potsdam, in the old Hohenzollern palace just outside the ruins of Berlin, the tensions between the wartime allies were becoming acute. This was not a replay of Yalta, in which personal appeals to wartime loyalty could carry much weight. Already, America's wartime leader had been replaced. Before the Potsdam conference was complete, Churchill had been voted out of office and replaced by Attlee, and the assertive role in the British delegation was now taken by the new foreign secretary, the veteran trade-union boss Ernest Bevin.

The negotiations over the outstanding issues of Poland and the other Eastern European countries proved difficult and divisive. As the new Secretary of State James Byrnes reported to the three leaders on 28 July: 'The US has unfortunately found that if it agrees with the Soviet delegation, the British delegation does not agree, and if it agrees with the British, then the Soviet disagrees.'[49] Potsdam papered over some cracks, on reparations and the decision to treat Germany as an economic unit, rather than as zones. But the mistrust which followed Yalta was not allayed, and it now festered in the transformed environment of the nuclear age.

Whatever Truman may have thought about Stalin's bland reaction to his low-key reference to the new weapon, it came as no surprise to the Soviet leader. In Ottawa on 9 July, a week before the New Mexico test, one of the British physicists on the project, Dr Alan Nunn May, met his contact, Colonel Zabotin, of the Soviet Embassy to Canada. He gave Zabotin '162 micrograms of Uranium 233, in the form of acid, contained in a thick lamina'. From Klaus Fuchs, another of the British scientists in the Manhattan Project, the Russians knew precisely what kind of weapon was being developed, and that the final manufacturing on the bomb was being carried out.[50]

The pressure was now on Stalin. The evening after Truman's casual remark, Stalin ordered Molotov to cable the chief Russian nuclear scientist Kurchatov to accelerate the work on the Soviet bomb project. Stalin then personally cabled Beria, the secret-police chief, with the same instruction.[51] In Bulgaria and Romania, the establishment of pro-Soviet governments was accelerated, and the pressure on Turkey began to permit the passage of Soviet warships through the Dardanelles. Although Stalin had agreed to withdraw Soviet troops from northern Iran by February 1946, preparations began for their reinforcement, along with the formation of a separatist movement in the Iranian province of Azerbaijan. Truman was 'worthless', Stalin confided to Nikita Khrushchev.[52] But the pace of events in the Far East was about to pass Stalin by.

The atom bomb was dropped on Hiroshima on 6 August, and the Soviet Union had yet to fulfil its Yalta promise and declare war upon Japan. Soviet troops were poised and straining at the leash to invade Manchuria, but the Chinese government was still prevaricating on the precise terms on which it would invite the Soviets to join the war. This was deliberate. Now that the Americans had the war-winning bomb, the need for Soviet allies, so powerful at Yalta, had passed. Byrnes, the Secretary of State, had already urged Truman to force the Japanese surrender without Soviet participation if possible. Stimson and General Marshall saw little point in further diplomatic efforts to bring in the Soviets now that the US had the war-winning weapon. From the Moscow Embassy, Harriman helped the Chinese delaying tactics.[53]

Aware that they faced a race against time if any of the spoils of war were to be won, the Soviet Union declared war on 9 August, the day the second atom bomb fell on Nagasaki. Two days later, when the Japanese offered to surrender, it was Stalin's turn to delay, hoping to bargain for Soviet influence over post-war Japan. The Allies should first 'reach an agreement' on the commanders and structure of the occupation, Molotov told Harriman just before dawn. 'I reject it in the name of my government,' Harriman retorted, without bothering to check with Washington.[54] Stalin dropped it, but noted sourly that the joint Allied occupation agreements that were in force in Vienna and Berlin were not being extended to the Russians in Tokyo.

'They [the USA and Britain] wanted to take advantage of the results of the war and impose their will not only on their enemy, Germany, but on their ally, the USSR as well,' Khrushchev concluded.[55] The Soviet view was understandable, and in Britain, in the American Embassy in Moscow, in the State Department, the OSS and among Truman's top military advisers, Khrushchev's suspicions were justified. But Truman's subsequent actions make it clear that the Roosevelt tradition of trust was not entirely dead. First, there is clear evidence of American demobilisation. The US Army numbered over eight million men at the time of Japan's surrender. Within the month, the GIs were being processed out of the army at the rate of 15,000 a day, 100,000 a week. By 1948, the army had been slashed to 554,030.[56] This was hardly evidence of aggressive intent. Second, there was intense debate in Truman's cabinet over whether or not to share the scientific secrets of the atom bomb with the Russians.

In the month after the atom bombs fell on Japan, Colonel Stimson went to his cabin in the Adirondacks to grapple with the new moral problem, to which he finally felt the only solution was the principle he had learned at the Skull and Bones club of Yale: 'The only way to make a man trustworthy is to trust him.' These were the closing words on the long memorandum, on the need to share with Russia the bomb's secrets, that he took to Truman on 12 September. 'If we fail to approach them [the Soviets] now, and merely continue to negotiate with them, having this weapon rather ostentatiously on our hip, their suspicion and their distrust of our motives and purposes will increase,' it argued. Stimson had already submitted his resignation, knowing that Secretary of State Byrnes was heading for a new meeting with Molotov, and 'wished to have the implied threat of the bomb in his pocket'. Truman persuaded Stimson to stay on until the next cabinet meeting on 21 September, when it would be the only topic on the agenda.[57]

After Stimson spoke, the new Under-Secretary of State Dean Acheson took up his argument: 'The advantage of being ahead in such a race is nothing, compared with not having the race.' Treasury Secretary Fred Vinson differed: military secrets should not be shared. The bulk of the cabinet agreed with Vinson. Truman, who had heard similar sentiments from the Congressional leaders, stressed they were 'not discussing the question of giving the secret of the bomb itself to the Russians or to anyone else, but the best methods of controlling bomb warfare and the exchange only of scientific information'.[58] Faced with a divided cabinet and watchful Congress, Truman devised the politician's compromise of an Atomic Energy Commission. The scientific principles were secrets no longer; they could be shared. But what he later called 'the know-how of putting it together' could not.[59] This was not Stimson's grand gesture of trust; but nor was it the Kremlin's image of the capitalist class warrior bent on atomic domination.

But if Soviet intelligence had access to the papers being drafted in the office of the joint chiefs of staff at the Pentagon, their worst suspicions would have been justified. In a paper entitled 'Strategic Vulnerability of Russia to a limited air attack', the JCS produced in October 1945 a plan to destroy twenty of the largest Soviet cities with atomic bombs. They included Moscow, Leningrad, Gorky, Tashkent,

Baku and Novosibirsk, although interestingly not Kiev in the Ukraine, apparently because it had been so devastated by the conventional war just ended. Military staffs are constantly producing contingency plans; that is their job. The importance of the 'Strategic vulnerability' paper should not be overrated, but the fact remains that just ten weeks after the end of World War Two, US military planners were contemplating the targets of World War Three.[60]

The choice of targets was explained as 'mixed industrial areas containing the highest proportion of research and development, specialized production facilities and key government or administrative personnel'. The strategic rationale of the Pentagon staff was spelt out with chilling clarity; these targets 'would exploit the maximum capacities of the weapon, produce the quickest, most direct and certain effects on Russia's immediate offensive capabilities, and achieve greatest impact against her latent offensive power'.

The great question remains: who was to blame for the Cold War? American revisionist historians have put the blame on their own side, on the determination to consolidate and extend US economic dominance, or at least on the distinct change of policy that came with Truman's inheritance of the White House. Post-glasnost Soviet scholars have pinned the responsibility squarely on Stalin and his imperial ambitions. Neither answer is persuasive. Leaders of great powers, amid wars and negotiations and the constant press of events, are seldom able to devise a coherent plan, or to apply it.

The Soviet Union had an ideology which gave the capitalist West ample cause to be nervous, and Russia had a history which mandated a suspicion of its neighbours. The implicit tensions in their relations might have been eased, as President Roosevelt had believed, by American goodwill. But Roosevelt died, and Truman had to prove himself fit to fill those giant shoes. Truman took the best advice on offer, and with the exception of Stimson and Wallace, the bulk of his cabinet, his diplomats and his Soviet experts urged him to be firm. Harriman, although he later claimed to have been on Roosevelt's side of the argument all along, certainly helped to steel Truman's resolve and intensify his suspicions in the crucial first days after he inherited the White House. It is just possible, had Roosevelt lived, and had there been no stricken Europe between them, no Western European Allies still festooned in embarrassing colonial entanglements, and in a most prickly pride, that the Cold War might not have got under way. But Roosevelt was dead, the Americans had the monopoly of the bomb and Europe sprawled between the victors, to be occupied, rescued or fought over.

The real culprit was the dreadful logic faced by both sides when they confronted the problem of what was to be done with defeated Germany. The dilemma was plain: to ensure that it could not start a third European war, but also to treat it fairly enough so that German resentment would not explode dangerously in the future, as it had done after the Treaty of Versailles in 1919. For Stalin, that meant occupation, and a defensive zone for the Soviet Union throughout Eastern Europe. For the West, it meant de-Nazification, free enterprise and stable democratic institutions, with the emphasis often on the stability rather than the democracy. But the problem of Germany, where both sides were prepared to be ruthless, led inevitably to the problem of Poland, where the West was touched by honour and sentiment and by domestic political considerations. Britain had gone to war for Poland in 1939, Polish pilots had tipped the balance in the Battle of Britain and Polish troops had fought loyally alongside the Allies in Italy and in France. And in the USA, Polish-Americans commanded seven million votes.

Roosevelt's admirable hopes for a post-war settlement based on the wartime Grand Alliance depended upon the maintenance of trust, which withered in the bitter disputes over Poland in that pre-nuclear summer between the conferences of Yalta and Potsdam. But Germany and Poland were only the most dramatic aspects of the much larger problem of Europe. Unconditional surrender meant Germany laid waste, Britain exhausted, France and Italy demoralised, and the whole continent of Europe prostrate. 'There is complete economic, social and political collapse going on in central Europe, the extent of which is unparalleled in history unless one goes back to the collapse of the Roman Empire,' John J. McCoy, Stimson's chief aide at the War Department, wrote to Truman on 23 April.[61]

Only Russia and the United States were in a position even to begin to grapple with the challenge. Neither one, it was soon clear, was prepared to let the other impose their different solutions: Sovietisation on the one hand, and the Marshall Plan on the other. The age-old issue of the control of Europe which had sucked Britain into so many interventions since the days of Churchill's ancestor, the first Duke of Marlborough, was beyond Britain's capacities. The Americans inherited the responsibility, and the role. And Europe's age-old question of the balance of power blended swiftly into the ideological struggle between capitalism and Communism. The two incompatible approaches to the problem of Europe were to become the competing visions of the wider Manichean struggle between the two mutually uncomprehending camps.

Chapter 2

Containment

They that dig foundations deep,
Fit for realms to rise upon,
Little honour do they reap
Of their generation.

'The Proconsuls', Rudyard Kipling

Hindsight imposes blinkers as well as perspective. From the viewpoint of the 1990s, there are few things harder to comprehend than the extraordinary popularity in the West by 1945 of 'Uncle Joe' Stalin and the heroic Red Army. For the American public, immune behind the Atlantic barrier, and for the British behind the Channel, there was something epic about the way the Red Army had borne the brunt of the fighting against Hitler's Wehrmacht, reeled back to the Volga, recovered at Stalingrad and fought their way back to Berlin. Until the US and British troops invaded Italy in 1943, they were facing only four divisions of German troops, while the Red Army grappled with more than two hundred.

Even for many conservatives, the pre-war memories of the evils of Communism had been redeemed by the blood the Red Army had shed in four years of war. The King of England presented a sword of honour to the fortress-city of Stalingrad. The British troops scrawled 'Joe for King' graffiti on Europe's ruined walls. And when he returned from victory in Europe, General Dwight Eisenhower solemnly assured Congress 'nothing guides Russian policy so much as a desire for friendship with the United States'.[1]

As wartime allies, the Russians were hailed as 'one hell of a people, who look like Americans, dress like Americans and think like Americans', by the later passionately anti-Soviet *Life* magazine.[2] This prime American weekly of its day, with a circulation of four million in the United States and another 317,000 abroad, went on to describe Stalin's secret police, the NKVD, as 'a national police similar to the FBI'.[3] Luce's business magazine *Fortune* ran an opinion poll in 1943 which found 81 per cent of the respondents agreeing that the US should work with Russia as equal partners in the coming peace.[4]

Look magazine ran an approving cover on 'A Guy Named Joe', which made Stalin into a friendly fellow: 'He knows Arctic meteorology, Leatherstocking Tales, soap and war.' He was also 'among the best-dressed of the world leaders, making Churchill in his siren suit look positively shabby'. *Collier's* magazine ran a special issue, 'What Kind of Country is Russia Anyway?' Neither socialist nor Communist, the magazine concluded, but 'a modified capitalist set-up . . . [moving] . . . toward something resembling our own and Great Britain's democracy'.[5]

America's political best-sellers of the day, *Mission to Moscow* by the former US Ambassador Joseph Davies and Wendell Wilkie's *One World*, contained breathtakingly indulgent accounts of Stalin's regime. Davies affirmed that in the show trials of Stalin's purges in the 1930s, 'justice had indeed been done'. Walter Lippmann, the most respected figure in American journalism, assured his readers that these two books were the most admirable studies of the Soviet Union on offer.[6]

The trust in Stalin which Roosevelt displayed at Yalta, and which Truman did not finally abandon until the year after the war's end, was not only widespread; it was a powerful political force. With 907,000 members in France by the end of 1945, and 1,771,000 in Italy, the Communists were the largest party in each country. The numbers swelled with the momentum and the respect that came from having been the spearhead of the French Resistance and the Italian partisans.[7] On 26 May 1946, in the last free elections Czechoslovakia was to hold for another forty-four years, the Communists won just over 35 per cent of the vote. This was more than twice as many votes as the next largest party, led by the veteran President Eduard Beneš.[8]

For many Europeans, the wartime feats of the Red Army blended with the still bitter memories of capitalism's failures during the Great Depression and the mass unemployment of the 1930s. In Britain, Churchill was swept from office in the general election of 1945 because the Labour Party's promise of a welfare state and a planned economy seemed to guarantee no return to those conditions. Central planning and state control had won the war, went the Labour Party argument of 1945. Now they could win the peace. 'To me, as to millions of others, Soviet behaviour after the war came as a bitter disappointment. We had thought, as Bevin told the Labour Party Conference in 1945, that "Left could speak to Left",' recalled Denis Healey, a Communist as an Oxford undergraduate in the 1930s, who went on to become the most pro-Nato defence secretary of the 1960s Labour government.[9] At Britain's 1945 election, some Labour candidates were introduced with passionate pleas for an Anglo-Soviet alliance.[10]

The speed with which Stalin's popularity was transformed into fear and contempt was a most remarkable swing of public opinion, and it is striking that the Soviet Union should on repeated occasions have provoked dramatic shifts of Western opinion. It happened in August 1939, when Stalin signed the Non-Aggression Pact with Hitler, the prelude to the German–Soviet partition of Poland. It happened again in 1956, when the invasion of Hungary devastated what was left of pro-Soviet opinion in the West, and in August 1968 with the invasion of Czechoslovakia, and again in December 1979 with the invasion of Afghanistan. On each occasion, a long and partially successful 'peace offensive' from Moscow was ruined by the sight of a great power asserting the prerogatives of its own security by sending its troops into the territory of a small neighbour.

And yet the Soviet Union was not just another great power, defending its interests with a mixture of force and diplomacy in the classic manner of international affairs. It could act with the selfish logic of the breed, signing the sphere-of-interest agreement with Churchill to carve up the post-war Balkans, just as Tsar Alexander I had sat with the Emperor Napoleon on a raft on the Niemen river to carve up Europe between them. But Stalin's USSR was also seen in the West as something different and more menacing, a unique and implacable ideology in arms, threatening to expand. This shift in perception took place among the governing establishments in both London and Washington in the last weeks of 1945 and the first two months of 1946. In the course of one hundred days, the West's view of the Soviet Union changed from an assumption that the Russian bear was up to its old tsarist tricks of dominating Eastern Europe and thrusting to the Dardanelles, into a conviction that the West was being conscripted into a new crusade. The syntax and vocabulary switched from the traditional lexicon of the balance of power to a language altogether messianic.

One American diplomat, George F. Kennan, played a remarkably powerful role in bringing this about. A shy, erudite and formidably intelligent man, Kennan had been a member of the first team of American diplomats to open diplomatic relations with the Soviet regime, and was to become, briefly, the US Ambassador to Moscow at the height of the Cold War. He was by no means an instinctive democrat. In the course of one of his periodic depressions, Kennan in

1938 drafted a book explaining why 'benevolent despotism' in America was to be preferred to the shrill disorders of democracy, and its core was the need for 'the very extensive restriction of suffrage in national affairs'. Immigrants, blacks and women (Kennan dubbed them 'frivolous') were to be denied the vote. From his earliest experiences of the Soviet state, Kennan in 1931 was writing of Soviet Russia as 'unalterably opposed to our traditional system, there can be no possible middle ground or compromise between the two . . . the two systems cannot even exist in the same world unless an economic cordon is put around one or the other of them.'

Kennan's bleak views were deepened by his experience of the purge trials of pre-war Moscow, and found some oddly Freudian roots. 'Nations, like individuals, are largely the product of their environment, and many of their characteristics, their fears and neuroses, as well as their abilities, are conditioned by the impression of what we may call their early childhood.' Russia's early childhood, Kennan noted, was the experience of the Mongol yoke. And it is difficult to escape the conclusion that Kennan's own gloom about Soviet Russia was linked to his own capacity for unhappiness. An intensely private, moody and introspective man, Kennan praised his Norwegian wife for 'the rare capacity of keeping silent gracefully. I have never seen her disposition ruffled by anything resembling a mood.'

A clever analyst, and deeply read in pre-Revolutionary Russian culture, Kennan was not a man to strike up much rapport with the Soviet officials with whom he dealt, far less to make personal inroads into the suspicious and hostile world of Moscow under Stalin's terror. Ironically, for the influence he was to wield on US–Soviet relations, Kennan had begun his diplomatic career in 1933 by recommending that 'We should have no relationship at all with them'. He did not like the Russians very much, or at least those workers and peasants in whose name the Revolution had been launched. On a visit to the Black Sea resort of Sochi, he confided to his diary:[11]

> Had the fathers of the Revolution really imagined that once the upper and middle classes had been kicked out of these watering places, the members of the proletariat would move in and proceed to amuse themselves gracefully and with taste? Did they really fail to foresee that such simple people would make pigsties of these hotels and villas, would have no appreciation for sky and air and mountain scenery?

As Ambassador Harriman's resident Soviet expert in the Moscow Embassy, Kennan's sombre and hostile views began increasingly to set the tone of Harriman's cables. Kennan despised the Yalta agreements as 'the shabbiest sort of equivocation', and mused about the possibility of Britain and the United States negotiating a separate compromise peace with Germany. In the post-Yalta summer of 1945, Kennan proposed the obvious solution for a man with such authoritarian leanings, to 'divide Europe frankly into spheres of influence, keep ourselves out of the Russian sphere and keep the Russians out of ours'. From his desk at the State Department, his former Embassy colleague Charles Bohlen retorted: 'Foreign policies of that kind cannot be made in a democracy. Only totalitarian states can make and carry out such policies.'[12] The history of the following year, whose tone was to be set by Kennan's famous long telegram, was to show how far democracies could be changed into accepting just such 'totalitarian' solutions.

In the months after the Potsdam conference, there was plenty of evidence for those who assumed that Stalin was conducting Russia's traditional expansionist policies. The foreign ministers of the Big Three met in London in September, and 'failed to agree on anything'. Britain's Ernest Bevin told his officials: 'Our relations with the Russians about the whole European problem are drifting into the same condition as that in which we had found ourselves with Hitler.'[13]

Bulgaria and Romania followed Poland in establishing servile pro-Soviet governments. Bulgaria did so with an improbable 88 per cent vote for the Fatherland Front, in elections which American diplomats insisted were rigged.[14] Another foreign ministers' meeting was held in Moscow in December, just as pro-Soviet forces in northern Iran seized control, and declared a new national government of Azerbaijan, which immediately granted the Soviet Union oil-drilling rights. The *New York Times* reported that Soviet troops had kept the Iranian army inside its barracks.[15]

On the following day, the same newspaper reported an intensified war of nerves against Turkey, with *Pravda* and *Izvestiya* announcing claims on Turkish territory by Soviet Georgia. This came against the background of an alarming buildup of Soviet divisions, with 200,000 troops in Bulgaria, and twelve divisions on Turkey's eastern frontier. The Soviet Union was pressing for open access for its warships through the Dardanelles, and for refuelling and repair facilities which sounded ominously like the nucleus of a naval base.[16]

In Washington, where the daily press reports and diplomatic cables began to take on the drumbeat of impending war, this was more evidence of the Kremlin's drive to expand and conquer. From the Soviet point of view, this was all balance-of-power politics as usual.

The Soviets had already swallowed their exclusion from the Allied governments in Italy and in Japan, although in justice Stalin could claim as much right to a voice in administering these defeated enemies as the United States was claiming in the governments of Eastern Europe.

As Molotov insisted, they were in Eastern Europe simply collecting the spoils they had been promised by Churchill in 1944, and ratified at Yalta and Potsdam. In the Dardanelles, they were pushing for the right of access to the Mediterranean, which had been a foreign-policy goal since the eighteenth century, and which Truman had acknowledged at Potsdam. In Iran and Turkey, they were pushing their traditional influence on the southern border. And they were doing so in a defensive mood. As Alexander Sokolov argued in *Novoye Vremya*, the Moscow current-affairs weekly, it all began with the US control of the atom bomb, which 'altered the views of some foreigners who formerly advocated international collaboration . . . [but now] . . . attempt to use the atom bomb in the game of international power politics'.[17]

The Soviets were playing the game as they had always understood it, from the classic experience of European diplomacy; push for advantage where one can, relax the pressure where one must. The war of nerves on Turkey had been relaxed on 2 November, when the Turkish government accepted the principle that Soviet warships had free rights of passage through the Dardanelles. When the US Secretary of State Byrnes came to Moscow in December to complain of the new regimes in Romania and Bulgaria, Stalin and Molotov accepted the American proposals to change their composition with little demur.[18] The following year, they were to back down in Iran as well.

Moreover, the Soviets felt aggrieved that their gestures of ideological concession were repeatedly ignored in the West. The Communist International, the organisation which subordinated all foreign Communist parties to Soviet authority, had been formally wound up in 1943. It had been done in terms which explicitly accepted that there were now various national routes to socialism, because of 'the deep differences of the historic paths of development of various countries'. The closing resolution of the Comintern said the organisation 'has been outgrown by the growth of the working-class movement, and by the complications of its problems in separate countries and has even become a drag on the further strengthening of the national working-class parties'.[19]

For the party faithful, including its leaders in Poland, Czechoslovakia, Bulgaria and other Eastern European countries, this acceptance of 'differences of historic paths' was to be taken seriously. The leader of the Greek Communist Party, Nicos Zachariades, returned from the Dachau concentration camp seriously seeking to cooperate with the British 'protectors', until the British backed the purge of the left by the right-wing government of Admiral Voulgaros. Bulgaria's Giorgi Dimitrov stressed that his country 'would not be a Soviet Republic'. Poland's Wladysaw Gomuka argued, in a theoretical journal intended for party members, not for the West, that 'the dictatorship of the working class, and still more of a single party, would be neither useful nor necessary'. The opening of the Czech party archives in 1968 found internal party documents from 1946 which make it clear that these were also the official views of the party leader, Klement Gottwald, who informed the central committee in September 1946 that: 'Comrade Stalin told me that experience has demonstrated, and the classics of Marxism–Leninism teach that there is not just the one path, through Soviets and the dictatorship of the proletariat.'[20]

An entire school of theory about the unique nature of the new peoples' democracies of Eastern Europe, where private property coexisted with state control of heavy industry, and Communist parties coexisted in pluralism with social democrats and peasant parties, was developed by the Soviet economist Eugene Varga, and published in Moscow.[21] 'It is possible to have political rule by the working people even while the outward forms of parliamentary democracy are still maintained,' Varga argued. His school did not flourish long. The 'outward forms' were to be viciously savaged in the party politics of Poland, Bulgaria and Romania, and in 1947, a deliberate process of political destabilisation and intimidation forced the collapse of the Smallholders Party government in Varga's Hungary. In March 1947, Varga came under criticism in *Pravda*, and by the following year his institute was closed.

The free elections of 1945 in Hungary had resulted in the Smallholders Party winning 57 per cent of the vote, followed by the United Front of Communists and Social Democrats with 34 per cent. The *New York Times* correspondent reported seeing less election day intimidation than in the machine politics of New York City.[22] For most of 1946, Varga's theory of a different and democratic path to socialism had at least some basis in reality. Varga even raised (if only to dismiss) an interesting parallel with Britain, where the new Labour government had established a not dissimilar economic system, nationalising the railway companies, the coalmines and the steel industry, and was building a state health service.

By 1947, these fledgeling hopes that a non-Soviet form of government might develop in Eastern Europe, with mixed economies and
parliamentary pluralism, were to be stubbed out, victims of the
greater confrontation in which they were to be pawns. And in the light
of that confrontation, and the ruthlessness which with Soviet rule was
later applied, the dreams of 'separate paths to socialism' looked worse
than naïve. But in the heady days of 1946, after the defeat of Fascism
and the thrill of liberation, idealism was in the air. And a degree of
guarded trust in Moscow's intentions was not always betrayed. In one
of the Soviet borderlands, where the intensity of Cold War confrontation was less sharp, the government of Finland was able to establish
a slowly increasing independence from Moscow, with a mixed economy and free institutions.

The last chance of such a political compromise for the countries of
Eastern Europe died in the final weeks of 1945, just at the moment
when the American Secretary of State Byrnes felt he had succeeded.
Stalin and Molotov had accepted his insistence that the governments
in Romania and Bulgaria be widened to include more opposition
ministers and non-Communists, and Byrnes said he felt that US
diplomatic recognition could now be extended to them. The Turkish
crisis was easing. Stalin easily approved Byrnes's proposal for a UN
commission on control of atomic energy. Byrnes, a former Supreme
Court justice and veteran Senator who had been senior to Truman in
the US Senate, was convinced he had reached a breakthrough, re-
establishing Roosevelt's wartime understanding with the Soviets.

His diplomats thought Byrnes had lost his senses. The entire US
legation staff in Romania threatened to resign at this 'sell-out'. From
the Moscow Embassy, Kennan wrote of 'fig leaves of democratic
procedure to hide the nakedness of Stalinist dictatorship'.[23] In Washington, the Republican Senate leadership was up in arms at the
thought of sharing atomic secrets with the Soviets. The *New York
Times* complained that nothing had been settled on Turkey and Iran,
and Truman was incensed at the lack of consultation with the White
House before Byrnes reached his agreements. Truman abruptly
ordered Byrnes to cancel his plans for a radio broadcast on his
diplomatic breakthrough until the Secretary of State reported back to
the President in person. Truman called Byrnes into the Oval Office on
5 January 1946, and in cold anger read aloud the text of a letter he had
drafted, a letter which has been seen as the real start of the Cold
War:[24]

At Potsdam we were faced with an accomplished fact and were by circumstances almost forced to agree to Russian occupation of eastern Poland, and that part of Germany east of the Oder river by Poland. It was a high-handed outrage. There isn't a doubt in my mind that Russia intends an invasion of Turkey and the seizure of the Black Sea Straits to the Mediterranean. Unless Russia is faced with an iron fist and strong language, another war is in the making. Only one language do they understand – 'How many divisions have you?' I do not think we should play compromise any longer. We should refuse to recognize Rumania and Bulgaria until they comply with our requirements; we should let our position on Iran be known in no uncertain terms . . . and we should maintain complete control of Japan and the Pacific. We should rehabilitate China and create a strong central government there. We should do the same for Korea. Then we should insist on the return of our ships from Russia and force a settlement of the Lend-Lease debt of Russia. I'm tired of babying the Soviets.

Truman subsequently described this letter in his memoirs as 'the point of departure of our policy'. It was not. It represented merely the high point of the first phase of Truman's evolving perception of the Soviet threat, the culmination of his growing suspicion that Stalin was determined to expand as far and as fast as the Red Army would permit. But the entire memorandum with its sweeping geographical references, its grandiose strategic positions, is couched in the vocabulary of the balance of power. And this was the vocabulary of a permanent American overseas commitment and an unending military expenditure which would prove difficult to sell to a US Congress and a fast-demobilising American public still thrilling to the novelty of peace.

The real point of departure came in the following month, when Truman's anger at the Soviet skill at tilting the balance of power gave way to the Manichean vision of a war between good and evil. It began with the elections to the Supreme Soviet, and Stalin's traditional eve-of-poll speech. Stalin knew there was no prospect of an American financial loan, that Lend-Lease was over, and that his other hopes of economic recovery were blocked by the British and American opposition to his requirements for reparations from Germany. Stalin also knew that Truman had failed to ratify Byrnes's promise to extend diplomatic recognition to Bulgaria and Romania. So the West's observers in Moscow expected that Stalin's speech would be bitter, and heard what they wanted to hear.

'The war was the inevitable result of the development of world economic and political forces on the basis of modern monopoly capitalism,' Stalin began. 'The capitalist system of world economy harbours elements of general crises and armed conflicts, and hence, the development of world capitalism proceeds not in the path of smooth and even progress but through crisis and the catastrophes of war.'[25]

This was boilerplate Marxism–Leninism, and Stalin went on to say that the World War Two alliance had assumed 'an anti-fascist and liberation character'. He said in vague and general terms that

> the unevenness of capitalist development usually leads in time to a violent disturbance of equilibrium, that group of capitalist countries which considers itself worse provided than the others with raw materials and markets usually making attempts to alter the situation and repartition the spheres of influence in its favour by armed force. The result is the splitting of the capitalist world into two hostile camps and war between them.

But Stalin did not attack the USA and Britain by name, nor did he say that a post-war slump in the capitalist West would pave the way for socialism. He warned that the need to rebuild Soviet industry would call for longer delays in consumer goods; for more five-year plans devoted to heavy industry. But if Stalin's speech was predicting international tension, the text is clear that it would be within the capitalist world, rather than against the Soviet Union.

This was not how the speech was reported in the United States, where *Time* magazine said it was 'the most warlike pronouncement uttered by any top-rank statesman since V-J Day'. Justice William Douglas told the US Naval Secretary Forrestal that this was 'the declaration of World War Three'.[26] The State Department's Paul Nitze, another Wall Street banker who entered government with the war and was to become one of the high priests of arms control, went to see Forrestal to warn him that this was Stalin's 'delayed declaration of war on the United States'. Others were less alarmed, instead rather baffled by Soviet behaviour, and by its increasing reluctance to cooperate in any international forum, including the economic systems of the World Bank and International Monetary Fund. Accordingly, the State Department and the US Treasury cabled the US Embassy in Moscow, asking it to shed some light on the background to Stalin's speech and the real motives of Stalin's foreign policy.

The cables went to Kennan, in charge of the Embassy since Harriman's departure. He was ill and depressed and thinking of resignation because his eighteen months of warnings about Stalin had gone unheeded. This was his chance. He dictated a 5,540-word cable which became known to history as the Long Telegram, and it struck Washington like a thunderbolt.

Carrying the official stamp 'not subject to condensation', it was forwarded in full to Byrnes, to Under-Secretary Dean Acheson, and then to Navy Secretary Forrestal who printed hundreds of copies for circulation throughout the Washington establishment. All State Department officers were sent a copy, and one of them noted:[27]

> It came at a moment when the Department, separated by circumstances from the wartime policy toward Russia, was floundering about, looking for new intellectual moorings. Now, in this communication, it was offered a new and realistic conception to which it might attach itself. The reaction was immediate and positive. There was a universal feeling that 'This was It', this was the appreciation of the situation that had been needed.

'USSR still lives on antagonistic "capitalist encirclement" with which in long run there can be no permanent peaceful co-existence,' Kennan's telegram began in the clipped syntax of the original cable.

> At bottom of Kremlin's neurotic view of world affairs is traditional and instinctive Russian sense of insecurity.
> Russian rulers have always feared foreign penetration, feared direct contact between Western world and their own, feared what would happen if Russians learned truth about world without or if foreigners learned truth about world within. And they have learned to seek security only in patient but deadly struggle for total destruction of rival power, never in compacts and compromises with it.

So argued Kennan, seeking the roots of Stalin's policies far back in Russian history. But then Kennan struck the new theme, that Stalin and his Communist predecessor, and thus presumably Stalin's heirs, would also be different and worse than even the most purblind of Russian Tsars, because on to the neurosis of old Russia was added the fanaticism of a new creed.

> Marxist dogma, rendered even more truculent and intolerable by Lenin's interpretation, became a perfect vehicle for sense of insecurity with which Bolsheviks, even more than previous Russian rulers, were afflicted. In this dogma, with its basic altruism of purpose, they found justification for their instinctive fear of outside world, for the dictatorship without which they did not know how to rule, for cruelties they did not dare to inflict, for sacrifices they felt bound to demand. In the name of Marxism they sacrificed every single ethical value in their methods and tactics . . .

Thus Kennan went on, defining the threat as the combination of the most brutal of great powers with the more ruthless of ideologies. Kennan's concept was to become the new orthodoxy of the West, and from the beginning, he nailed it to immediate diplomatic reality by forecasting the war on many fronts that the West now faced.

In the Western powers

> efforts will be made to hamstring measures of national defence, to increase social and political unrest, to stimulate all forms of disunity . . . poor will be set against rich, black against white, young against old, newcomers against established residents etc.
>
> Violent efforts will be made to weaken power and influence of Western powers [on] colonial, backward or dependent peoples. On this level, no holds will be barred.
>
> Where individual governments stand in path of Soviet purposes pressure will be brought for their removal from office.
>
> In foreign countries Communists will, as a rule, work towards destruction of all forms of personal independence – economic, political or moral.
>
> Everything possible will be done to set major Western powers against each other. Anti-British talk will be plugged among Americans, anti-American talk among British. Continentals, including Germans, will be taught to abhor both Anglo-Saxon powers.
>
> In general, all Soviet efforts on unofficial international plane will be negative and destructive in character, designed to tear down sources of strength beyond reach of Soviet control . . . we have here a political force committed fanatically to the belief that with US there can be no permanent modus vivendi, that it is desirable and necessary that the internal harmony of our society be disrupted, our traditional way of life be destroyed, the international authority of our state be broken, if Soviet power is to be secure.

This was more than a call to arms, it was an invitation to a life-and-death struggle in which there would be no quarter given on either side. The confrontation with this implacable force of evil could not even be conducted on logical terms, since Kennan went on to argue that Soviet policy 'is seemingly inaccessible to considerations of reality in its basic reactions'. It did not even believe in the existence of objective truth: 'This government is actually a conspiracy within a conspiracy; and I for one am reluctant to believe that Stalin himself receives anything like an objective picture of the outside world.'

But having electrified Washington with this nightmarish spectre, Kennan offered a rationale for an American policy to confront it – 'the problem is within our power to solve – and that without recourse to any general military conflict'.

'Impervious to logic or reason, it is highly sensitive to logic of force' was his first argument; Western resolve could hold the line. Second, the Soviets were 'by far the weaker force'. Third, the 'success of Soviet system, as form of internal power, is not yet finally proven'. Finally, the West's own capacity for growth and self-improvement was the crucial bulwark against the terrible enemy – 'World communism is like malignant parasite which feeds only on diseased tissue'. Although the concept of 'containment' was not to be elaborated as the West's policy until Kennan published his anonymous article in *Foreign Affairs* the following year, its lineaments were already clear. The West had the physical and moral resources to resist Communism, and to outlast it, if it could only summon the political cohesion and will.[28]

Kennan's telegram was circulating in Washington as another crisis was brewing over Soviet troops and ambitions in northern Iran. They were eventually to withdraw, but when they bluntly refused to do so on 1 March, this implicit threat to the oilfields of the Middle East appeared to confirm Kennan's darkest forebodings. For the energy-sufficient USA, this was a matter of important strategic interests. For Britain, it was close to economic life and death. From 1945 to 1950, the Anglo-Iranian oil company generated $1.125 billion in profits, and paid more in taxes on its profits to the British government than Iran received in royalties.[29] The time was fitting for the delivery of the British echo to Kennan's telegram, and it came from the most respected voice of the day, Winston Churchill. No longer prime minister, but still the embodiment of the bulldog, Churchill travelled with Truman to the President's home state to deliver what became known as the 'iron curtain' speech on 5 March 1946.[30]

'From Stettin in the Baltic to Trieste in the Adriatic, an iron curtain has descended across the continent,' Churchill warned, citing territory and political influence, in the classic terms of European diplomacy. 'All are subject, in one form or another, not only to Soviet influence but to a very high and increasing measure of control from Moscow.' But Churchill then went on to endorse Kennan's argument, that this was a rampant ideological threat, even more than the predictable expansion of a great power.

> Far from the Russian frontiers and throughout the world, Communist fifth columns are established and work in complete unity and absolute obedience to the directions they receive from the Communist centre. Except in the British Commonwealth and the United States, where

Communism is in its infancy, the Communist parties or fifth columns constitute a growing challenge and peril to Christian civilisation.

The fame this speech and phrase acquired has obscured the fact that it was not well received in public at the time. While Truman had endorsed Churchill's sentiments by sitting alongside him, applauding and nodding during the delivery, Truman later told reporters he had not known what Churchill was going to say, and replied 'no comment' when they pressed him for a reaction. The American press was critical of Churchill's suggestion of an alliance, 'a fraternal association of the English-speaking peoples'. To Walter Lippmann, the leading commentator of the day, the speech was an 'almost catastrophic blunder', the leftist *Nation* dubbed it 'remarkably inept'. The *Wall Street Journal* assumed Churchill was seeking an Anglo-Saxon alliance against the Soviet Union, and disapproved: 'The country's reaction to Mr Churchill's Fulton speech must be convincing proof that the US wants no alliance, or anything that resembles an alliance, with any other nation.'[31]

If the American press was less than impressed, Churchill was speaking precisely the language of US officialdom. The week after his speech, the Joint Chiefs of Staff at the Pentagon forwarded to the White House a solemn strategic appraisal of the implications of the Iranian crisis which concluded: 'The defeat or disintegration of the British Empire would eliminate from Eurasia the last bulwark of resistance between the US and Soviet expansion . . . Militarily, our present position as a world power is of necessity closely interwoven with that of Great Britain.'[32]

The sheer pace of events now became a factor in the way that official Western opinion was hardening against Stalin. It was barely two months earlier that Truman had snapped at Byrnes that he was 'tired of babying the Soviets'. The Kennan telegram had since given Truman a rationale, Churchill had provided a ringing phrase, and the Pentagon furnished a strategic argument. Events then moved even faster. The day the Pentagon report was completed, there were two reactions in Moscow. The first came from Stalin, and the second was the British Embassy's own version of Kennan's telegram. Stalin's response came in an interview with *Pravda*, saying that Churchill's speech was 'a dangerous move, calculated to sow the seeds of dissension among the Allied states'.[33] Stalin had two main points to make: the first was offensive, that Churchill embodied British imperialism and a racist supremacy as odious as that of Hitler's Nazis; and the second defensive, that the Soviet Union's role in Eastern Europe was misunderstood.

'Mr Churchill sets out to unleash a war with a racial theory,' Stalin went on. 'The English race theory leads Mr Churchill and his friends to the conclusion that the English-speaking nations, as the only superior countries, should rule over the rest of the nations of the world.' Then came Stalin's defence: 'What can there be surprising about the fact that the Soviet Union, anxious for its future safety, is trying to see to it that governments loyal in their attitude to the Soviet Union should exist in these countries?'

Stalin's reaction in turn provoked Britain's acting Ambassador (and later Ambassador to the United States), Frank Roberts, to draft his own three equivalents of the Kennan cable. They followed one upon another, on 14, 17 and 18 March, landing back on Ernest Bevin's desk in London as a coordinated salvo. Less doom-laden that Kennan, Roberts was much cooler in his key conclusions: 'There is infinitely less danger of sudden catastrophe with the Russians than with the Germans . . . [and] . . . they do not call for open conquest and least of all for the launching of a war of aggression, except possibly for limited aims.'[34] But the same apocalyptic note was there, as Roberts warned: 'It may even be asked whether the world is not now faced with the danger of a modern equivalent of the religious wars of the 16th century, in which Soviet communism will struggle with Western social democracy and the American version of capitalism for domination of the world.'

Even more striking for what it says about the attitude of mind in the West's Moscow Embassies as the Cold War got under way was a brief passage on the Russian national character. Kennan had written bitterly of the Russian historical legacy, and of his dismay at the behaviour of the proletariat in the Black Sea holiday resorts; Roberts went further, suggesting 'a fundamental streak of laziness, indiscipline and inefficiency running through the Russian people, who must be constantly kept up to the mark if they are to preserve their position in the world'. This was the authentic British voice of the imperial pro-consul, complaining of the feckless ways of his charges. Add this to Kennan's historicist gloom, and it is clear that the Western establishments were getting some odd, as well as hostile, perspectives on the nature of the Soviet threat from their representatives in Moscow.

By the end of March, just a year after Yalta, the new, combative approach had taken hold in Washington and London. But it was only an approach, an attitude based on reaction to what was seen as Soviet aggression, and which now was sustained by the intellectual cohesion of Kennan's telegram. It had not yet become a coordinated policy, and far less was there a readiness to develop a military alliance, or even to sustain and develop the West as one loose economic unit. There was little political will for rearmament; the British were already desperately overstretched to maintain the garrisons of Empire, reintroducing conscription in October 1946. The Americans, and to a lesser degree the British, were inspired to be negative, to block Soviet moves, rather than to build something more positive in response.

But the new firmness was clear in March 1946 in Truman's insistence in what he called 'a blunt message' that Soviet troops leave Iran. Truman's threat, backed up by Britain, was to join a formal Iranian complaint in the United Nations; it had no teeth. The joint chiefs had made it clear they could contemplate military action in Iran 'only in the event of mobilisation for general war'.[35] But the Soviets, apparently sensitive to assembled opinion at the UN, withdrew.

Heartened by this success, Bevin and Byrnes, the British and American representatives at the council of foreign ministers meeting in Paris in April jointly blocked every Soviet proposal. The Soviets would not be allowed to join a four-power control system over the Ruhr; they would not be permitted large reparations from Germany and its former allies; Yugoslavia's claim on Trieste was rejected; and most ominously from the Soviet point of view, Byrnes pressed for something new, the removal of all trade preferences across Eastern Europe.

To the Americans, this demand for 'equal economic opportunity', which they repeated at the next foreign ministers' session in June, was wholly routine. The objective of 'the enjoyment by all States . . . of access on equal terms to the trade and raw materials of the world' had figured in the original Roosevelt–Churchill Atlantic Charter of 1941.[36] But for the Soviet government, this American call for 'the open door' was suddenly interpreted as something close to a declaration of capitalist war by other means. The new Soviet Ambassador in Washington, Nikolai Novikov, drafted his own version of Kennan's long telegram in September 1946.[37] It stressed that

> the countries of Europe and Asia are experiencing a colossal need for consumer goods, industrial and transportation equipment etc. Such a situation provides American monopolistic capital with prospects for enormous shipments of goods and the importation of capital into these countries – a circumstance which would permit it to infiltrate their national economies. Such a development would mean a serious strengthening of the economic position of the US in the whole world and would be a stage on the road to world domination by the US.

By the time he wrote this cable, Novikov certainly knew of the sacking of Vice-President Henry Wallace, one of the few voices in Truman's cabinet calling for moderation and a return to President Roosevelt's wartime alliance with Stalin. Novikov did not know that the suspicions of Truman's White House had already moved on to a new stage. In July 1946, Truman had asked his aide Clark Clifford to draft a speech, the keynote of a campaign to educate the American public in the nature of the Soviet threat. Clifford asked his assistant George Elsey to prepare the draft, and Elsey consulted Kennan. The final version was handed to Truman on 24 September, and Truman asked for all ten copies to be given to him and kept under lock and key, saying, 'This is so hot, if this should come out now it could have an exceedingly unfortunate impact on our efforts to try to develop some relationship with the Soviet Union.'[38]

'If we find it impossible to enlist Soviet cooperation in the solution of world problems, we should be prepared to join with the British and other Western countries in an attempt to build up a world of our own . . . recognizing the Soviet orbit as a distinct entity with which conflict is not predestined but with which we cannot pursue common aims,' the Clifford–Elsey paper argued.[39]

Truman used this theme that 'Conflict is not predestined' in his speech to the United Nations General Assembly the following month, stressing, 'This is still one world, compact and indivisible.' As he left the podium, a delighted Molotov rushed up to shake his hand. On the same day, Stalin announced further cuts of 80 billion roubles in the Soviet defence budget, and an acceleration of demobilisation. Returning the troops to civilian life almost as fast as the United States, the Red Army shrank from the 1945 peak of almost 12 millions to 3 million men by 1948.[40]

These were hopeful signs, and to understand what confounded these signs of mutual hope it is important to realise the economic difficulty which aggravated the ideological and strategic tensions. On the original version of the Novikov cable, released from Soviet archives only in 1990, there are a series of ticks and marks and underlinings, all in the hand of foreign minister Molotov. He underlined the passage about 'the importation of capital', and leaned heavily on the Novikov cable for his speech at the Paris peace conference in October 1946. Molotov's objections to the 'open door', and to the invasion of Western cultural and economic influence this would invite, have an oddly prophetic ring today:[41]

It is surely not so difficult to understand that if American capital were
given a free hand in the small states ruined and enfeebled by the war, as
the advocates of the principle of 'equal opportunity' desire, American
capital would buy up the local industries, appropriate the more attract-
ive Rumanian, Yugoslav and all other enterprises, and would become
the master in these small states. Given such a situation, we would
probably live to see the day when in your own country, on switching on
the radio, you would be hearing not so much your own language as one
American gramophone record after another or some piece or other of
British propaganda. The time might come when in your own country,
on going to the cinema, you would be seeing American films sold for
foreign consumption.

  Is it not clear that such unrestricted applications of the principles of
'equal opportunity' would in practice mean the veritable economic
enslavement of the small states and their subjugation to the rule and
arbitrary will of strong and enriched foreign firms, banks and industrial
corporations? Was this what we fought for when we battled the fascist
invaders?

In Molotov's eyes, the United States had begun waging its economic
war almost as soon as Truman took office, when the Lend-Lease ships
were first turned back, and when the Soviet application for trade
credits was 'lost' in Washington bureaucracy. In the wake of the
Kennan telegram, the first sign of the new American militancy which
reached Molotov was a State Department memorandum of 21 February 1946. It warned him that any negotiations on credits would
have to take account of compensation claims by American owners for
their holdings in the Soviet-occupied areas of Europe and Manchuria.
This paper repeated the American insistence on an open door for
trade, and said the United States should be consulted and represented
on all matters to do with economic reconstruction in Eastern Europe.
It also gave notice that the United States wanted to negotiate a Soviet
settlement of its debt for Lend-Lease supplies.[42]

  There was a degree of innocence in the American position. Funds
had been appropriated for the Export–Import Bank, in the expectation that trade credits would be extended to Moscow. But in March
1946, the French premier Léon Blum and his financial adviser Jean
Monnet arrived in a Washington still feverishly discussing the Kennan
telegram, and they warned that without economic support, their
government was likely to fall and be replaced by Communists. The
French received the money instead, with $2.7 billion of war debts
written off, and an American guarantee of a further $1.3 billion for
the French trade deficit. France was rescued in the name of anti-

Communist solidarity, while Poland, Czechoslovakia and Hungary had their credit applications rejected at the World Bank. Secretary Byrnes explained the matter bluntly: 'The situation has so hardened that the time has now come, I am convinced, in the light of the attitude of the Soviet government and the neighbouring states which it dominates, [that] we must help our friends in every way and refrain from assisting those who either through helplessness or for other reasons are opposing the principles for which we stand.'[43]

By the end of 1946, the senior officials in Washington were convinced that they had to contend with an implacable and expansionist Communist state, well-armed, secretly policed, and utterly ruthless, and commanding the resources of client states in Eastern Europe. The senior officials in Moscow were equally convinced they had to contend with an America, supported by Britain and client states in Western Europe, which had its own implacable plan for economic penetration and dominance of the globe. The more each side became convinced of its image of the other, the more they were locked into hostility.

The event which was to seal this hostility into permanence was, ironically, an act of nature. As the suspicions of 1946 hardened into enmity, and as Kennan and Roberts and Novikov established their new orthodoxies in their respective capitals, the weather intervened. The harvest of 1946 was terrible across Europe, and the winter of 1946–7 was the harshest in living memory. The economic crisis in Europe, which had been appalling in 1946, became critical in 1947, and forced the United States to take direct responsibility for the fate of its cold and hungry friends in Europe. Even before a wave of blizzards struck Britain in January, the government had been forced to cut coal supplies to all industries by half. Unemployment rose to six millions, double the peak of the Great Depression of the 1930s, and electricity was limited to a few hours each day. Food rationing was more severe than it had been during the war. The $5,000 million in loans extended by the United States and Canada in 1945 was being exhausted at what the Treasury called 'a reckless and ever-accelerating speed'. Keynes had warned the Americans that this would follow their insistence that the pound be convertible.[44]

Too poor to hang on, but too proud to let go, Britain had clung by its fingertips to the traditional status and commitments of a great imperial power, with its troops and ships stationed around the world. The terrible winter of 1946–7 proved too much, and the commitments had to go. India's independence would have to come within the year, the Palestine mandate would be handed to the United Nations, and the economic and military defence of the eastern Mediterranean would have to be surrendered.

On the gloomy Friday afternoon of 21 February 1947, the British Ambassador's secretary rang the State Department, asking for an urgent meeting with the new American Secretary of State, General George Marshall, the legendary wartime chief of staff. Marshall was out of town, but suspecting what was coming, acting Secretary Dean Acheson arranged to receive a copy of the formal 'blue paper' so that its implications could be addressed by the time Marshall returned on Monday. The British first secretary, Henry Sichel, delivered two documents to Loy Henderson, the State Department's head of Near Eastern Affairs.

'They were shockers. British aid to Greece and Turkey would end in six weeks,' Acheson later recalled. 'The British could no longer be of substantial help in either. His Majesty's government devoutly hoped that we could assume the burden.'[45]

Acheson began a flurry of weekend activity to prepare papers, cost estimates and recommendations, and celebrated on Sunday evening with martinis with Loy Henderson and a toast to 'the confusion of our enemies'. Marshall approved, persuaded President Truman and the War and Navy Secretaries, and on 26 February Truman convened the crucial meeting at the White House with the Congressional leaders who would have to vote the funds. The mid-term elections of November 1946 meant that the Democrats no longer controlled Congress. The Republican Senators and Congressmen, among whom the tendency to isolationism was almost instinctive, would have to be persuaded that the frontiers of US security were now on the Dardanelles. 'I knew we were met at Armageddon,' wrote Acheson, and after Marshall gave a leaden report, Acheson took over. As he recalled:[46]

> These Congressmen had no conception of what challenged them. It was my task to bring it home. Soviet pressure on the Straits, on Iran and on northern Greece had brought the Balkans to the point where a highly possible Soviet breakthrough might open three continents to Soviet penetration. Like apples in a barrel infected by one rotten one, the corruption of Greece would infect Iran and all to the east. It would also carry infection to Africa through Asia Minor and Egypt, and to Europe through Italy and France, already threatened by the strongest domestic Communist parties in Western Europe. The Soviet Union was playing one of the greatest gambles in history at minimal cost.

After the long silence which followed this performance, Senator Arthur Vandenburg, the powerful Republican whose support was required for a bipartisan foreign policy, said to Truman: 'Mr President, if you will say that to the Congress and the country, I will support you and I believe most of its members will do the same.'[47]

This was the birth of the Truman Doctrine, formally spelt out to the joint session of Congress by the President on 12 March. Truman successfully called for $400 million in aid for Greece and Turkey, and for the right to send US troops to administer the reconstruction and train local forces. But far more important for the future was the much wider principle Truman established. He drew a distinction between two worlds, of freedom and coercion, of free institutions against terror and oppression.[48]

> The seeds of totalitarian regimes are nurtured by misery and want. They spread and grow in the evil soil of poverty and strife. They reach their full growth when the hope of a people for a better life has died. We must keep that hope alive. I believe that it must be the policy of the United States to support free peoples who are resisting attempted subjugation by armed minorities or by outside pressures.

The impact of that savage winter of 1947 did not stop with Greece and Turkey. British poverty was serious, France was equally beset, but the western zones of Germany were in the worst plight of all. Divided by the zones of the four powers, and restricted from developing the old nucleus of its heavy industry in the Ruhr, Germany was prostrate, and the cities close to starving. The costs of occupying Germany drained over $300 million from Britain in 1946. The French wanted to annex the Saar as a way to guarantee their coal supplies, and the Soviet government was able to exploit these divisions of Western policy.

For the American zone commander, General Lucius Clay, the solution was plain; the German economy had to be freed from the constraints of occupation. For Truman, this made sense, so long as the Republicans in Congress would agree, and to ensure that they did, Truman asked the former Republican President Herbert Hoover to visit Germany and make his own report. Hoover agreed with Clay, and so did the future Republican Secretary of State John Foster Dulles, who called for expansion of the German economy within a united Europe.[49] That made the policy bipartisan. But the strategic decision to revive, or perhaps unleash once more the German economy, was guaranteed to alarm the Soviet Union. Even some Germans warned that this might be going too far, too fast. 'Russia can point to the enormous damage Germany has already caused, and could do again if rebuilt,' noted Rudolf Kustermeier, the Social Democrat editor of *Die Welt*.[50]

Both the French and the Russians had a veto over changes in Germany as a whole. The reluctant French could be made to agree, through the prospect of further US economic support. The Russians could not, and at the foreign ministers' council meeting in Moscow, Molotov refused to soften Soviet demands for reparations from Germany. But the British and Americans refused to pump support into the Western zone of the German economy if the Russians were simultaneously pumping it out of their zone. Molotov hoped he could block the entire proposal. And since Molotov was conducting these negotiations with General Marshall while the US President was announcing the Truman Doctrine, the division of the world into the free and the enslaved, the Soviet refusal to yield was understandable.

The only Anglo-American alternative was to proceed on their own, dragging the French along, and beginning the process of what was to become the forty-year division of Germany into East and West. The Truman Doctrine, the Dulles speeches and the Hoover report all pointed to a way in which Germany could be rebuilt, while reassuring France and the other Western European countries so recently under German occupation. But even as the awful winter of 1947 gave way to spring, there was no time to waste. US Under-Secretary of State Will Clayton made a swift tour, and reported in May: 'Millions of people in the cities are slowly starving . . . Without further prompt and substantial aid from the US, economic, social and political dislocation will overwhelm Europe.' As General Marshall said in a radio address to the American people after returning from Moscow, 'The patient is sinking while the doctors deliberate.'[51]

Walter Lippmann, dean of American journalists, perceived the inevitable implication. On 5 April, Lippmann's 'Cassandra Speaking' column argued that to fend off a crisis which threatened to 'spread chaos throughout the world, political and economic measures on a scale which no responsible statesman has yet ventured to hint at will be needed in the next year or so'. Three weeks later, Lippmann spelt out the logic that linked the Truman Doctrine to what would become the Marshall Plan: 'After we have discussed the separate needs of Britain, France, Italy and the rest, we should suggest to them that they meet together, agree on a general European program of production and exchange, of imports and exports to the outer world, and that they arrive at an estimate of the consolidated deficit for as much of Europe as can agree to a common plan.'[52]

The Marshall Plan for the recovery of Europe was formally unveiled in a speech at Harvard University on 5 June 1947. Marshall stressed that: 'It would be neither fitting nor efficacious for this government to undertake to draw up unilaterally a program designed to place Europe on its feet economically. This is the business of the Europeans. The initiative, I think, must come from Europe.'[53] Acheson ensured that it did, briefing three British journalists on its importance, and advising them to tell their editors to send full copies of the speech to Ernest Bevin at the Foreign Office. Bevin immediately telephoned Georges Bidault, the French foreign minister, and within two weeks, they and the Russian foreign minister Molotov were all meeting in Paris.

The American press did not see Marshall's speech as quite so important. In the next day's *New York Times*, the first headline read, 'Truman Calls Hungary Coup "Outrage" ', the second headline went on, 'Demands Russians Agree to Inquiry', and only the third headline said, 'Marshall Pleads for European Unity'.[54]

Molotov was invited because the Marshall Plan was designed to seize the moral high ground for the West. The Truman Doctrine speech had made US attitudes to Moscow coldly clear. But if the Marshall Plan were to fail, the Soviet Union should be seen to be responsible. Accordingly, Marshall stressed in his Harvard speech: 'Our policy is directed not against any country or doctrine but against hunger, poverty, desperation and chaos. Its purpose should be the revival of a working economy in the world so as to permit the emergence of political and social conditions in which free institutions can exist . . . Any government which manoeuvres to block the recovery of other countries cannot expect help from us.'

It was the task of Bevin and Bidault to ensure that Molotov understood the political implications of Marshall's phrase about 'free institutions'. But Molotov had come to Paris with more than a hundred experts, including economists, transport and logistics consultants and even nutritionists. Moscow, it was clear, was seriously interested in Marshall's offer, if the terms were right. Molotov began by saying each European country should add up its financial needs, and send the combined list to the Americans. That, retorted Bevin, would be asking for a blank cheque. 'Debtors do not lay down conditions,' Bevin added.

Molotov suspected that like the 'open door' trade policy, the Marshall Plan would be the Trojan Horse of the American dollar, a way to infiltrate the Soviet Union and its sphere of influence in order to destroy it. He suggested that 'only allied countries that had suffered from the ravages of war should participate'. This would exclude both Italy and Germany. Bevin and Bidault said no. Trying to force a decision, Bevin then offered a proposal for a steering committee to draw up a programme for four years, and listing what Europe needed, and what it could provide. Bevin suggested Britain, France and the Soviet Union, and four other European countries should sit on the committee. This was insurance against being outvoted if Communist ministers should block the plan in the French government.

Molotov objected again, saying there 'must be no infringement of the national sovereignty of the European states'. He was then handed a telegram, only partially decoded, straight from Moscow. It reinforced Molotov's hard line; Stalin would not accept common planning, with its implication of American and British economists poring over the Soviet economy. In effect, the Paris conference was over. The Marshall Plan, Molotov finally declared,[55]

> has now served as a pretext for the British and French governments to insist on the creation of a new organisation, standing above the European countries and intervening in the internal affairs of the countries of Europe . . . The European countries will lose their former economic and national independence to the advantage of certain strong powers . . . It will lead to Britain, France and the group of countries that follow them separating from the rest of Europe, which will split Europe into two groups of states.

In this, Molotov was absolutely right. But then Britain and the non-Communist parties in France and the other Western European countries had already chosen their sides. If the Iron Curtain were indeed falling across Europe, then all but the socialists and those to their left knew on which side they preferred to be. On 4 July, two days after Molotov's departure, Bevin and Bidault invited twenty-two European governments, all except Fascist Spain and the Soviet Union, to a wider conference in Paris the following week. The Czechs, Poles and Hungarians all agreed, Bulgaria and Albania expressed interest, and only Yugoslavia and Romania said they would first consult with Moscow.

Moscow cracked the whip. The Czech premier Klement Gottwald and foreign minister Jan Masaryk were summoned to Moscow on 8 July, to be threatened with grim consequences should they go to Paris. Masaryk glumly observed that he had gone to Moscow as the minister of a sovereign state, and returned as a Soviet lackey.[56] Poland, Romania, Yugoslavia, Bulgaria, Albania, Hungary all rejected the invitation, and so did Finland. In retrospect, this has been defined as the moment when the Soviet boot crushed itself into the face of Eastern Europe. At the time, the implications were not so clear.

'Could we risk a complete break with Moscow?' pondered Hubert Ripka, the Czech minister of foreign trade, and a socialist rather than Communist. 'The Soviets might well incite the Communists, in that case, to effect a coup d'état. We were unfortunately unable to expect effective help from the Western powers.' But then Ripka made a different, telling point, citing 'another reason, still more serious. I know that we could not win over the majority of the people for such a policy.'[57]

Ripka was pointing to the uncomfortable truth that whatever the opinions in the White House and Kremlin, many of the people of Europe were still torn. There was as yet no clear division between Communists and non-Communists in Europe. Denis Healey, then the international secretary of the British Labour Party, and by now a firm anti-Communist, spent the year of 1947 attending a series of socialist party conferences across Europe, watching these fraternal parties split between those who wanted to maintain a united front with the Communists, and those prepared to join the liberals and moderate conservatives against the Communists. Eastern Europe was an odd mix of pluralism and putsch. Healey was in Hungary in January 1947 when one of the few Social Democrats in the political police was shot in the back from a Russian limousine. But he also attended the last free conference of Czech social democrats in November of that same year, when the party voted to reject a proposal for fusion with the Communists.[58]

The full weight of Soviet rule did not fall until the following year, with the Communist putsch in Prague in February, and the suicide (or murder) of Jan Masaryk on 10 March. His body was found in the courtyard beneath his window in the foreign ministry. Even in November, Masaryk had few illusions of what was coming, telling an old friend that Czech Communists had already been given orders 'to liquidate their political opposition'.[59] The orders had been given at the first meeting of the Cominform, the Communist Information Bureau, which Stalin launched on 22 September 1946 as a direct response to the Marshall Plan. He convened a conference of the leaders of the Communist parties of Poland, Czechoslovakia, Yugoslavia, Romania, Hungary, Bulgaria, France and Italy, to be the

replacement of the unlamented Comintern. This was the formal end
of Eastern European hopes of differing paths to socialism.

The report to this extraordinary assembly of European Communists was delivered by Andrei Zhdanov. It contained five main themes.
The first was that 'America's aspirations to world supremacy
encounter an obstacle in the USSR, the stronghold of anti-imperialist
and anti-fascist policy'. The second was that war was not inevitable –
'Soviet foreign policy proceeds from the fact of the co-existence for a
long period of the two systems, capitalism and socialism'. The third
was that time was not on the West's side: 'World War Two aggravated
the crisis of the colonial system, as expressed in the rise of a powerful
movement for national liberation in the colonies and dependencies.
This has placed the rear of the capitalist system in jeopardy.' The
fourth was that 'The Truman Doctrine, which provides for American
assistance to all reactionary regimes which actively oppose the democratic peoples, bears a frankly aggressive character.' And the fifth,
designed to summon the memory of Nazism, was that: 'The corner-
stone of the Marshall Plan is the restoration of the industrial areas of
Western Germany controlled by the American monopolies.'[60]

The Italian Communists were stunned by the sharpness of the
ideological turn. They were even more dismayed by the attack made
by the Yugoslavs upon the Italian and French Communists for not
having had the courage to try to seize power in 1945, even though this
policy had met with Moscow's approval at the time.[61] The Communists of Western Europe were henceforth conscripted into Soviet
service, to be flung as shock troops against the Marshall Plan. As
Zhdanov stressed: 'If they are prepared to take the lead of all the
forces prepared to defend the cause of national honour and independence in the struggle against attempts to subjugate their countries
economically and politically, then no plan for the subjugation of
Europe can succeed.'[62]

The result was a wave of strikes, street demonstrations and battles
with the police in France and Italy, throughout the winter of 1947–8.
Two million workers struck in France on 18 November, the red flag
was raised over the Palais de Justice in Marseilles, and the main trade-
union body, the Confédération Générale du Travail, formally condemned American aid to France. Parliamentary proceedings were
virtually halted, but the government of Robert Schuman stood firm.

The strike called to stop the Paris Métro failed in December, and the wave receded. It lasted longer in Italy, but failed there too, in part because the US and Canadian food aid had begun to arrive in Europe.[63]

But another factor now came into play, the new institutions of national security being established in the United States. On 19 December 1947 the first of them, the National Security Council, held its first meeting in Washington, and decided to use the equally new Central Intelligence Agency to run covert operations in Europe. One of the first directives passed that day, titled NSC 4/A, ordered Admiral Roscoe Hillenkoeter, the new director of Central Intelligence, to use covert methods to prevent a Communist victory in Italy.[64]

The immediate target was the elections of the following year. The methods used included propaganda, disinformation, secret payments to non-Communist political parties, public threats to withhold US aid from a Communist government, and special training and equipment to the Italian armed forces. This was not the beginning of the secret war. That can be dated back to the last days of the war against Germany, when Frank Wisner of the OSS, and later of the CIA, began negotiations with Reinhard Gehlen, the former head of Fremde Heere Ost, the German Army's formidable intelligence department which covered the Soviet armed forces. Gehlen's files and skills and agents were swiftly put at American disposal.

But the Italian crisis represents the first political decision from the White House to launch the secret war. The stakes were recognised to be high. From his new post at the State Department in Washington, Kennan cabled to the US Embassies in Europe: 'Italy is obviously key point. If Communists win election there, our whole position in Mediterranean, as possibly in Europe as well, would probably be undermined.' And if the Communists should win, Kennan recommended US military intervention.[65]

In retrospect, the congealing of the Cold War in 1947–8 was oddly like a series of volleys in a tennis match. The United States opened the service by proposing the Marshall Plan. The Soviets returned the serve by convening the Cominform, and launching the strikes to stop it. The US rushed food to Europe to beat the strikes. Realising their Western European effort had failed, the Soviets responded by establishing firm control in Eastern Europe with the coup in Czechoslovakia. The West's reply was to militarise what had hitherto been an economic relationship with Western Europe. The armed camps began to mobilise under their two opposing banners.

'It really has become a matter of the defence of Western civilisation or everything will be swamped by this Soviet method of infiltration,' Bevin told the British cabinet.[66] The Brussels Defence Pact, of Britain, France and the Benelux countries, was agreed that month. Under its terms, Britain agreed to come to their defence against invasion, and to keep troops in Germany for fifty years. On 12 March, two days after the death of Masaryk in Prague, General Marshall called in the British Ambassador in Washington. 'Please inform Mr Bevin that we are prepared to proceed at once in the joint discussions on the establishment of an Atlantic security system,' Marshall said. Ten months after his launch of the Marshall Plan, the North Atlantic Treaty Organisation was under way.[67]

If the firmness of this Western response came as a surprise to Moscow, a further shock was in store. Unable at first, and later unwilling, to get American credits, and barred from rebuilding its economy through wholesale looting of the western zones of Germany in the name of reparations, Soviet economic recovery was now dependent on whatever resources it could mobilise in its own sphere of influence. Already restive at this, and unwilling to plunge into massive investments in heavy industry, the Communists of Yugoslavia under the wartime partisan leader Marshal Tito began increasing their trade with the West. Yugoslavia also took the lead in proposing a Balkan Federation, which would include a customs union with Czechoslovakia and Poland.

At first, it seemed a routine matter of party discipline. Bulgaria and other Eastern European countries dropped the idea as soon as Moscow complained. But Yugoslavia bridled. On 18 March 1948, hoping to exert sufficient pressure for the Yugoslav party to evict Tito and change the policy, Stalin began to withdraw the Soviet military and economic advisory teams. But Tito, as much a nationalist as a Communist ideologue, began negotiating if not to join the Marshall Plan, then at least to become a fellow traveller. He succeeded. By 1951, the US had supplied Tito with $150 million in civilian aid, and another $60 million in arms.[68]

While the vicious polemics between Stalin and Tito did further damage to what remained of pro-Soviet sympathies among Europe's non-Communist left, the real implication of the Marshall Plan began to unfold. In February, British, French and US officials met in London to discuss a joint plan for the reindustrialisation of their zones of

Germany, treating all three as a single unit. On 7 June, the London Recommendations called on the premiers of the West German provinces, the Länder, to convene a constitutional assembly, which led to the West German state. And on 18 June, the currency reform and the birth of the Deutschmark was announced. The division of Europe was complete, save for the two isolated cities of Vienna and Berlin, still inside the Soviet zone. On 23 June, the Western powers announced that the Deutschmark would also be introduced into their sectors of West Berlin, and on the following day, the Soviets announced their blockade of the city.

Open war, or at least direct military confrontation, was very close. The American General Clay proposed sending US armoured columns into the Soviet zone to clear the roads, a suggestion supported by the fiery British left-wing Labour MP Aneurin Bevan, so much had Stalin lost credibility in the West. The wiser head of Ernest Bevin prevailed, along with the logistical skills of the US Air Force Generals Hap Arnold and Curtis LeMay who recalled how 72,000 tonnes of supplies had been flown over the Himalayas into China during World War Two. And the unprecedented Berlin airlift began. It lasted for eleven months, fed two million people and delivered enough coal to stop them freezing through the winter.[69] An astonishing display of the West's industrial weight and political determination, it also sealed into place the strategic permafrost which was to settle over Europe for a generation.

Not all the aircraft were flying into Berlin. On 18 July, two US Air Force groups of sixty B-29 'atomic bombers', equipped to deliver nuclear weapons, flew into their new British bases. The atom bombs, it later emerged, did not join them until the outbreak of the Korean War in June 1950. Deliberately, however, widespread publicity was given to the bombers' arrival, even though it is doubtful whether the US arsenals contained as many as fifty atom bombs for them to drop, and it is unlikely they would all have been committed to the British-based force.[70] It was all done very briskly and even casually, without any formal treaty.

'Never before in history has one first class power gone into another first class power's country without an agreement. We were just told to come over and "We shall be pleased to have you",' recalled the bombers' commander, General Leon Johnson.[71] That was only a part of the implication of the arrival of the bombers. Although the first

Soviet atom bomb test was not to take place until September of the following year, the nuclear stand-off over a divided Europe had begun.[72]*

* The declassification of parts of the Pentagon's official *History of the Strategic Arms Competition, 1945–72*, in 1993, finally fills in some of the gaps of public knowledge. The atom bombs in Britain, as elsewhere throughout the world, were under the custody of the Atomic Energy Commission, rather than the US armed forces. It was only in July 1950, with the outbreak of the Korean War, that President Truman authorised the storage of eighty-nine sets of non-nuclear components in Britain. The bombs' nuclear cores, the plutonium capsules, were still under the control of the AEC, in accordance with the provisions of the Atomic Energy Act of 1946. These nuclear and non-nuclear components of the bombs were not to be mated together, ready for use, until a full-scale war alert. The Defense Department was first authorised to hold both nuclear and non-nuclear components together in April 1951, when President Truman assigned nine Mark 4 'Fat Man' bombs to the personal custody of General Hoyt Vandenbergh, Air Force chief of staff. Authority to deploy complete warheads to Britain, under USAF custody, was not granted until April 1954. The British, at least, were informed of this. The French were not consulted when President Truman authorised the storage of non-nuclear components at SAC bases in French Morocco in January 1952.[73]

Chapter 3

The Cold War Goes Global – and Comes Home

> Our one task was known;
> Each to mould the other's fate as he wrought his own.
> To this end we stirred mankind till all Earth was ours
> Till our world-end strifes begat wayside Thrones and Powers,
> Puppets that we made or broke to bar the other's path,
> Necessary, outpost-folk, hirelings of our wrath.
>
> *'France', Rudyard Kipling*

The Cold War started in Europe because it was there that US and Soviet troops met in May 1945, over the corpse of Nazi Germany, and discovered that their concepts of Europe's post-war future were dangerously incompatible. Their deepening confrontation spread more slowly to the rest of the world, and without that hostility in Europe might never have spread at all. The United States found itself unhappily but increasingly supporting and then supplanting its European allies' colonial pretensions in Asia and Africa. And Stalin found himself equally glumly forced to support the Chinese Communist Party's successful struggle against the US-backed government of Chiang Kai-shek.

Once under way, once the idea of the Cold War had seized the minds of the leaders in Moscow, Washington and London, it took on a strange kind of creativity, leading them into actions which had never been thought out, but which had far-reaching effect. The American and British plan for post-war Germany had been harsh, to keep the Germans tamed, disarmed, de-Nazified and inhibited from rebuilding their formidable industrial machine. The combination of British poverty and the Soviet threat made that policy redundant within three years of Yalta. Germany had to be rebuilt, at first as an industrial base to help stabilise Western Europe, and then as a full-scale military ally. A similar process developed in Japan.

The initial plan for occupied Japan was to break its will and capacity for future aggression, to disarm the country, to break up the industrial combines, and to inculcate democratic values. The Cold War in Europe, and its spread to mainland China, forced a reassessment. By 9 October 1948, President Truman approved a recommendation from his new National Security Council, which declared that Japan's prosperity was deemed a Western strategic asset, and the policy goal henceforth was: 'To ready democratic Japan for entry into the free world's community of nations as a self-supporting trading partner.'[1]

Once the United States and the Soviet Union began to perceive one another through the prism of the Cold War in Europe, they saw that jaundiced image of the other wherever they looked. The irony was that Europe, the crucible, remained edgily at peace; the vast bulk of the Cold War's fighting and dying took part in Asia, the Middle East, Africa and Latin America. People with brown and black and yellow skins paid the price of what had begun in Europe as a white men's quarrel. But there was one important parallel between the post-war development in Europe and in Asia; the problems of the peace followed logically from the geographical locations the various armies of the Grand Alliance had reached in the course of winning the war. The defeat of Japan required the wresting of control from the Japanese armies all along the Asian littoral, from Manchuria and Korea in the north, to Burma in the Indian Ocean. And Japan had been fighting two rather different kinds of war. The first, which Japan had been waging against China since 1931, was a classic war of imperial conquest. But the second, which Japan launched in December 1941, was not only an attack on American positions in the Pacific Ocean, it also assumed some of the characteristics of a war of Asian liberation against the European colonial empires in Asia.

The Dutch in Indonesia, the French in Indo-China, the British in Hong Kong, Malaya, Burma and India, and to a degree the Americans in the Philippines, each found that their experience of initial defeat at Japanese hands complicated their subsequent reoccupation. The British had been startled by the success of the Japanese in raising a small army of Indian prisoners of war under Subhas Chandra Bose to fight against them. After the war, the British were to be embarrassed by the hostility of the Indian public to the trial of Bose's men for treason. 'India adores these men,' said Gandhi, while Pandit Nehru, the first prime minister of independent India, hailed their 'passionate desire to serve the cause of India's freedom'. On 8 September, the French began their campaign to recover control of Vietnam from the local Communist resistance led by Ho Chi Minh, by releasing 1,700 Japanese POWs to fight on the French side. The American sense of confusion became acute when Ho Chi Minh began the Vietnamese Declaration of Independence with an approving quotation from the equivalent American Declaration of 1776.[2]

The United States became caught in a contradiction. American anti-colonial sympathies may have rested with the local nationalists, with whom in Vietnam, Indonesia and the Philippines they had fruitfully cooperated in the war of resistance against a Japanese occupation whose cruelty swiftly destroyed its initial welcome. But America's crucial allies in Western Europe demanded American support in reasserting control over their old Asian empires. And increasingly as the Cold War deepened they were able to do so not in the name of the old imperialism but in the cause of the new anti-Communism. The USA refused to help the Dutch recover their empire in the East Indies and threatened to withdraw Marshall Aid if the Dutch persisted; was gratified that Britain's Labour government sensibly granted independence to its Indian empire in 1947; but was to be haunted for a generation by the legacy of the French struggle and subsequent defeat in Indo-China. And when Americans followed the French into Vietnam, they were to misapply the lessons of fighting a Communist insurgency which the British had devised in retaining their control of Malaya.

In Europe, because of the Yalta agreements and the positions the Soviet and Western troops had reached in 1945, the Cold War had a static quality. In Asia, because of the civil war in China, and the replacement of the Japanese by the returning European colonialists, the situation became far more fluid and thus intrinsically far less stable. Ironically, both the United States and the Soviet Union had tried to establish stability in China. At the Dumbarton Oaks meetings in August 1944, the Soviets had accepted that Chiang Kai-shek's China would be one of the 'Big Five' members of the United Nations Security Council, with a veto. The next year at Yalta, Roosevelt had persuaded Stalin to agree to treat the nationalist government of Chiang Kai-shek as an ally, even though it had been fighting against Mao Tse-tung's Chinese Communists since 1927. Chiang and Stalin signed a Treaty of Friendship and Alliance in August 1945.[3]

As the war ended in China, it had been assumed by Stalin and the US alike that Chiang's forces would occupy the vast vacuum in northern and eastern China left by the Japanese defeat. Although nominally outnumbered five to one by Chiang's forces, Mao did not agree. The Chinese Communist Party had never enjoyed the wholehearted support of Stalin, and Mao acted under the assumption that he could defeat Chiang and his American supporters, but would have to rely on his own resources. Mao replied to the news of the treaty between Chiang, his civil-war rival, and Stalin, his ideological 'comrade', by telling his troops: 'Relying on the forces we ourselves organise, we can defeat all Chinese and foreign reactionaries.'[4]

China was filled with different armies. The Soviets swept through Manchuria and into northern Korea. The Americans established a naval base at Tsingtao, and by the end of 1945 there were 50,000 US Marines in the country. The British returned to Hong Kong, and Chiang Kai-shek resolved to use his new relationship with Stalin to assert control of the north. Stalin equivocated, allowing the Communists to seize vast stocks of captured Japanese arms, and Chiang's troops became increasingly overextended as they tried to take over the main towns of Manchuria from the Soviet troops. There was sporadic fighting between Chiang's forces and the Communists, and America's General Marshall tried and failed to organise a truce and a coalition government in which Chiang would have the dominant role.[5] The stakes, General Marshall asserted, could hardly have been higher. His mission was to fend off 'the tragic consequences of a divided China and of a probable Russian reassumption of power in Manchuria, the combined effect of this resulting in the defeat or loss of the major purpose of our war in the Pacific'.[6]

Corruption in Chiang's government combined with low morale among his troops and a devastating inflation to weaken what had looked like a commanding position. Newly armed from the Japanese stocks, and with some limited and covert Soviet support, Mao's armies began to win, in spite of Chiang's grudging American support. As President Truman recalled it,[7]

> Chiang Kai-shek decided he was going to occupy North China and Manchuria. General Marshall argued against it, and General Wedermeyer argued against it, but he went ahead. We furnished him equipment, money and a water-lift to Manchuria, and he sent the best divisions he had, well-trained and well-armed, to Mukden. They stayed there until finally the whole thing disintegrated, and they surrendered.

By the end of 1946, it was plain to General Marshall and to President Truman that to save the Chiang government in China, the United States 'would virtually have to take over the Chinese government . . . It would involve the US in a continuing commitment from which it would be practically impossible to withdraw'. In November, the US Seventh Fleet was ordered to withdraw the US Marines. The United States continued to supply Chiang with a total of $2 billion in economic and military aid as the civil war intensified, but with fading hopes that the Nationalist government would endure.[8]

The Cold War in Europe, deepening the conviction in Washington that the West faced a relentless global challenge by Soviet-led Communism, made Mao's advances look far more sinister. Dean Rusk, the deputy Under-Secretary of State for the Far East, and experienced enough to have understood the underlying tensions between Mao and Stalin, still saw it in terms of the spreading Soviet menace: 'Most of us saw Chiang Kai-shek's fall coming, but we were still disappointed when it happened. I saw it as a great tragedy, that the Chinese people, with their tremendous energy and potential, were now wedded to Communist ideology and allied with the Soviet Union.'[9]

There were abundant signs that this was not the case. In April 1949, when the Chiang government fled its working capital of Nanking, most of the world's Ambassadors remained. Only the Soviet envoy joined Chiang in the rout to Canton.[10] Mao proclaimed the People's Republic of China in October 1949, and in December went by train to Moscow, where he remained for two months, while the Sino-Soviet Treaty of Friendship and Alliance and Mutual Help was negotiated and signed. This was seen in the alarmed West as the fusion of a monolithic Communist block, dominating most of Eurasia. China's formal diplomatic recognition in January, while Mao was still in Moscow, of Ho Chi Minh's Vietminh as the legitimate government of a Vietnam still largely under French control, reinforced the Western fears.[11]

But the terms of the Sino-Soviet Treaty were significantly modest. They required the two countries to aid one another in war only in the event of Japanese aggression, or attack by 'any other state which should unite with Japan directly or indirectly in acts of aggression'. The most likely cause of war, an attack upon the Chinese mainland by Chiang's Nationalists from their fortress island refuge of Formosa (Taiwan), with or without US support, was clearly not the kind of conflict which would mandate Soviet support. And since Japan was disarmed, and equipped by the US occupation forces with a constitution which required that it remain disarmed, this was a treaty which did not pledge the Soviet Union to do very much at all.[12]

The revival of Japan came about through three accidents. The first was the decision of General Douglas MacArthur, known as SCAP (Supreme Commander, Allied Powers), to ignore the draconian Morgenthau plan for post-war Japan, and impose his own more lenient scheme. The second unforeseen development was the triumph of the

Chinese Communist Party, which transformed Japan from an occupied enemy into a Cold War bastion, whose need to strengthen its economic base led to the revival of the 'zaibatsu' industrial groups. The third accident was the Korean War, for which Japan was the American military and economic base.

MacArthur was granted extraordinary powers in 1945, which he exercised as a benevolent dictator – on his allies as well as on the Japanese. The Soviets were barred from any governing role in Japan akin to the four-power system in occupied Germany. The British were told that they would no longer command the Australian troops, that the 40,000 British and Commonwealth troops would be made part of the US Eighth Army, and that they too would join the Soviets in the purely consultative councils which MacArthur proceeded to ignore. His own troops were not forbidden to fraternise with the defeated Japanese, but were warned that they faced five years in military prison for striking or slapping a Japanese civilian. The US Ambassador to Japan, William Sebald, was stunned to learn that MacArthur's powers were such that the Ambassador's own cables back to the State Department had to be approved by SCAP.[13]

MacArthur informed the transitional prime minister, Kijuro Shidehara, that all legislators who had been members of militarist parties had to be dismissed from the Diet, the Japanese parliament. The prime minister said that meant the entire cabinet would have to resign. MacArthur said that was fine. The resignations were withdrawn. On 15 September 1945, the liberal newspaper *Asahi Shimbun* suggested in an editorial that the use of the atom bomb on Hiroshima and Nagasaki had been a breach of international law. It was closed for two days, but SCAP began weekly lectures for the Japanese press on the rights and duties of a free press.[14]

MacArthur required a new and democratic constitution. The Japanese government's draft was inadequate, and he wrote his own, an amalgam of British and American practice which established three separate branches of government and a parliamentary democracy. Above all, in Article IX, MacArthur's new Japanese constitution declared that the nation would by fundamental law 'forever renounce war as a sovereign right of the nation . . . Land, sea and air forces, as well as other war potential, will never be maintained.'[15] MacArthur's staff at SCAP included a number of 'New Deal' Democrats who brought their own social-democratic sympathies to the new Japan.

The Communist Party was legalised, and trade unions encouraged. In October, two months after the surrender and just one week after the demobilisation of the Japanese army, SCAP issued a directive which abolished all controls on religious, political and civil liberties, and gave women the vote for the first time. Land reform split up the great estates and gave the land to peasants. Informed by the 'New Deal' theories of the 1930s, MacArthur and his aides imposed a liberal constitution and social revolution on Japan. And they did it in a spirit remarkably free of wartime vengeance. Whereas in the US zone of Germany almost one in four of the population was 'screened' for de-Nazification, in Japan barely three per cent of the Japanese population went through similar procedures.[16]

MacArthur's early rule sought to fulfil the spirit of the idealist Atlantic Charter in whose name the Allies claimed to have fought. But he established political freedoms in desperate economic circumstances. Japan had suffered many fewer casualties than Germany in the war: 1,270,000 military dead, and at least another 670,000 civilians, of whom 138,890 died at Hiroshima alone. The figures are in dispute. Japanese estimates of civilian dead range up to two million. The Japanese economy had, however, been devastated. While Germany had coal and iron ore in the Ruhr, the Japanese islands had few raw materials for industry. The week after he arrived in Tokyo, MacArthur cabled back to Washington for 3.5 million tonnes of food. When Washington delayed, MacArthur sent a second dispatch: 'Give me bread or give me bullets.'[17]

At the end of 1945, Japanese industrial production was just 16 per cent of the level in 1940. With so little economic activity beyond the subsistence level, few taxes could be collected. The eleven great families, who had traditionally owned the giant zaibatsu, were forced to trade in their stocks for non-negotiable government bonds, and the salaries of the new managers were sharply restricted. In 1945, industrial production fell by 64 per cent. In 1946, it fell by a further 38 per cent. The year 1947 saw the first signs of recovery, with a 15 per cent increase, but from such a desperately low base that industrial activity was still just half of what it had been in 1934.[18]

To try to keep some industry alive, MacArthur scrapped the initial plans for reparations: to dismantle 1,100 Japanese plants and remove them to allied countries. It was not enough. When the first moderate socialist government was elected in 1947, there were just four days' supply of rice in the government warehouses. The growth of the Communist Party led to industrial militancy, and on 1 February 1947 a general strike was called. Already under criticism in the US press and Senate for introducing socialism to Japan, MacArthur banned the strike, and began to change course.[19]

For once in the post-war Japan he ruled, the new policy was not MacArthur's decision alone. The echoes of the Cold War in Europe helped impose it, and a retired head of the American Bankers' Association, Joseph M. Dodge, was brought out to Japan to execute the new course. The plans to dissolve the 1,200 firms which had been targeted in the Deconcentration Law, the vehicle to dismantle the zaibatsu, were deliberately delayed by the Japanese, and not pushed by the Americans. Dodge also began working to change MacArthur's ban on foreign investment into Japan. Back in Washington, Dodge had powerful supporters in the US Treasury, which was worried about the costs of MacArthur's policies. The price of sustaining the Japanese economy was rising sharply, from $108 million in fiscal year 1945–6, to $294 million in fiscal year 1946–7.[20]

The new American policy, based upon geo-strategic fear of Communists, was expressed with great frankness by US Army Secretary Kenneth Royall, in a speech to the Commonwealth Club of San Francisco, on 6 January 1948:[21]

> It is clear that Japan cannot support itself as a nation of shopkeepers and craftsmen and small artisans any more than it can exist as a purely agricultural nation. We can expect continuing economic deficits in Japan unless there is some degree of mass industrial production. We are building in Japan a self-sufficient democracy, strong enough and stable enough to support itself and at the same time serve as a deterrent against any other totalitarian war threats which might hereafter arise in the Far East.

As Royall spoke, the civil war in China was still being fought, but the Communists were evidently winning. In Europe, the Marshall Plan was under way. Japan was no longer an isolated group of islands, a problem unto itself and the American occupation. It was part of the global confrontation, taking its place in the West's battle line. Barely a year after the MacArthur constitution had banned a Japanese army, MacArthur was persuaded of the need for a 'jietai', or Self-Defence Force, of initially 75,000 men.

The speed with which America transformed its view about the kind of Japan it wanted can be traced not only to the developments in Europe and China, but also to a rising mood of panic in the United States. 'Our reaction to the fall of China in 1949 was that of a jilted lover,' Dean Rusk commented.[22] It was worse than that. The 'loss' of China was seen as a portent of eventual defeat on a global scale. 'The fall of China imperils the US,' General MacArthur wrote in *Life* magazine. *Time* brooded darkly on 'the red tide that threatens to engulf the world'.[23] The mood is caught in the preamble to the Internal Security Act, widely known as the McCarran Act, which was passed the following year: 'World Communism has as its sole purpose the establishment of a totalitarian dictatorship in America, to be brought about by treachery, infiltration, sabotage and terrorism.'[24]

This was to be the start of a curious pattern in the way that, towards the end of each decade of the Cold War, the West went through a crisis of morale, fearing that it was losing the great struggle. In spite of the formation of the Nato alliance and the steady success of the Marshall Plan in Europe, the loss of China cast a pall over the late 1940s. A decade later, the Soviet technological success with the launch of the first 'Sputnik' earth satellite led to accusations of a 'missile gap'. In the late 1960s, the combination of military setbacks in Vietnam and riots in the USA and across Western Europe and in Japan seemed to portend another going down of the West. And in the late 1970s, defeat in Vietnam combined with economic stagnation, US embarrassment in Iran and the Soviet invasion of Afghanistan to suggest yet another mood of imminent Western defeat.

In such moods, when the cry turns quickly from 'the nation in danger' to 'we are betrayed', democracies can react in uncharacteristic and terrible ways. The moral case for the cause of the West in its ideological crusade had been put simply and eloquently in the Truman Doctrine. He had talked of two worlds, one free, and the other living in fear of the boot through the door in the early hours of the morning. There were tragic times in the West when democratic governments sullied Truman's decent claim by acting in similar, unsavoury ways. The crisis of morale over the loss of China was to be one of the worst such times. It had begun earlier, with the entirely justified fears of spying. Soviet agents were indeed trying to find what they could of the Manhattan Project, and the West's atom-bomb secrets. It would have been extraordinary if they had not. But this was not a simple case of great powers spying upon one another, as they always had. The ideology of Communism, and the West's counter-ideology of freedom, each claimed to supersede the calls of national loyalty among the adherents.

The great difference was that at least in the 1940s, when it still enjoyed the nuclear monopoly, the West had more to conceal, and above all, the Soviets had started to recruit their intelligence networks much earlier. Understanding well how the West worked, the Communist spymasters exerted their greatest efforts, and were to achieve their greatest success, at the great and traditional universities of Oxford and Cambridge in the 1930s. With considerable forethought, the recruiters perceived that clever and ambitious and radical young undergraduates, if caught early, could be made to serve throughout the glittering and influential careers for which Oxford and Cambridge trained their élite youth.

The Cambridge group, based around an intellectual club named 'the Apostles', produced at least four important Soviet spies. They were Kim Philby, who was the official British liaison officer with US intelligence in Washington as the Cold War intensified, and rose to be deputy head of MI6, the British intelligence arm; Donald Maclean, who served in the Foreign Office, and photocopied top secret documents for Moscow from at least 1938, and was chief aide to the postwar British Ambassador in Washington, Lord Inverchapel; Guy Burgess, the flamboyant homosexual who escaped to Russia with Maclean in 1951; and Anthony Blunt, who served in MI6 in the war, and later became the curator of the royal art collection. The attractions of Oxford and Cambridge for young Americans in the 1930s brought an American connection to this network. Michael Straight, later editor of the *New Republic* magazine, finally confessed his participation in 1963, in the course of the FBI security check required when President Kennedy asked him to run a federal agency to encourage the arts. There was also a similar and parallel Oxford group, whose work has just begun to emerge from the Soviet archives.[25]

It is clear that Maclean and Philby helped Soviet intelligence in its efforts to penetrate US nuclear secrets, and the discovery of their work cast a long shadow over the intimacy and trust between the British and American intelligence operations which had been forged in the war against Hitler, and continued throughout the Cold War. But the use of Americans as Soviet agents, whether in the nuclear field or the more mundane spheres of the economy and general diplomacy, gave the American spy mania of the 1940s a hysterical and deeply politicised character.

On 3 August 1948, with the Berlin airlift under way and Chiang Kai-shek's armies reeling back to southern China, the House Committee on Un-American Activities called a *Time*-magazine editor, Whittaker Chambers, to testify under subpoena. Chambers said that he had been a Communist from 1924 until 1937, and in the course of his underground work had met a series of American officials. They had since risen to senior positions, and he could identify them as Communist agents or resources. Among others, Chambers named Harry Dexter White, who had become assistant secretary at the US Treasury, and Alger Hiss, a State Department official. Hiss had attended the Yalta conference as an aide, had helped organise the conferences at

Dumbarton Oaks, and been the secretary-general of the founding sessions of the United Nations at San Francisco.

'So strong is the hold which the insidious evil of Communism secures upon its disciples,' Chambers told the hushed Congressmen, as he described the moment he decided to leave the party, 'that I could still say to someone at that time "I know I am leaving the winning side for the losing side, but it is better to die on the losing side than to live under Communism." '[26]

The confrontation between these two Americans, Chambers from the Communist underground and *Time* magazine, and Alger Hiss of Harvard Law School and the State Department, dramatised the issues of the Cold War for the American public in an extraordinary way. The charges and countercharges went on for years, as Hiss denied the accusations but then acknowledged that he might have met Chambers, sued him for libel and lost the case. Hiss was then tried and imprisoned for perjury, still protesting his innocence of treason, while Chambers produced ancient papers typed on Hiss's typewriter from a hiding place in a pumpkin on his farm. The prolonged Hiss–Chambers affair popularised and Americanised the ideological issues behind the Cold War, and licensed unscrupulous politicians to launch Red witch-hunts throughout American society.

The Cold War entered the popular culture. Take Hollywood's classic movie of the Red Menace, *I was a Communist for the FBI*. It was made in 1951, based on the true story of Matt Cvetic, who had infiltrated the Communist Party in Pittsburgh. The film poster said it all, our hero pointing as his girlfriend is beaten up and kidnapped in an alley by his party comrades: 'I had to sell out my own girl – so would you.' It won an Oscar nomination for best documentary.[27]

Look magazine ran a cover story, 'Could the Reds Seize Detroit?' The Catechitical Guild Educational Society, a religious group based in Minnesota, printed and distributed four million copies of a comic titled *Is This Tomorrow? – America under Communism*. The Bowman Gum Company, famous for its baseball cards, brought out a new set of cards to go with its chewing-gum in 1951. Called 'Children's Crusade against Communism', its slogan was 'Fight the Red Menace'. Card 35 showed police bursting into an apartment. The text read:[28]

Why is this Russian family being arrested? Perhaps the radio is a clue. These people may have been listening to the Voice of America. The Voice, you know, is a radio program in which our State Department tells the truth about the free world. The Red leaders do not want the Russian people to learn what real freedom is like. They might ask it for themselves. But who reported that this family tuned in on the

Voice? Perhaps someone they thought was a friend. Who can tell who may be a spy for the secret police?

The politician whose name became most linked with the witch-hunts for Communists was Senator Joe McCarthy, who claimed to have lists of varying numbers of Communists in the State Department, in the Pentagon, in the army and other institutions of the state. His drinking habits, and the increasing wildness of his accusations, served to discredit him when leading figures who had too long been silent, like General Marshall and President Eisenhower, finally stood up to his bullying and slanderous tactics. But the Congressman who really began the process, cultivated Whittaker Chambers as a witness and led the prosecution of Alger Hiss, was the one leading politician in the West who can claim to have been in at the birth and death of the Cold War.

Richard Nixon had served in the US Navy during the war, and returned to his native state of California to run for Congress. 'The Hiss case brought me national fame,' Nixon later wrote.[29]

> I received considerable credit for spearheading the investigation which led to Hiss's conviction. Two years later I was elected to the US Senate and two years after that General Eisenhower introduced me as his running mate to the Republican national convention as 'a man who has a special talent and an ability to ferret out any kind of subversive influence wherever it may be found, and the strength and persistence to get rid of it'.

Nixon, and Senator Joe McCarthy after him, and with J. Edgar Hoover's FBI as their tool, unleashed a kind of intellectual and political civil war in the West. Some Republicans tried to make this a party matter. Congresswoman Clare Booth Luce charged that the Communist Party 'has gone underground, after the fashion of termites, into the Democratic Party'. But the Democrats were too cautious to permit this cleavage to take place along party lines. President Truman appointed the first commission to review the loyalty of civil servants. And it was the Democratic Attorney-General, Tom Clark, who told the Cathedral Club of Brooklyn on 15 January 1948: 'Those who do not believe in the ideology of the United States, shall not be allowed to stay in the United States.'[30]

By comparison with Stalin's Gulag, this was a soft repression, but it cannot have felt that way to Hollywood screenwriters and university academics and diplomats whose careers and livelihoods were deliberately disrupted. And the vicious effect of the febrile anti-Communism was publicly and resolutely challenged. The radical journalist I. F.

Stone was in the forefront of these American dissidents for civil liberties. 'In our milder fashion, we are continuing the practice of the "purge",' he observed. 'Though so far only Communists have gone to jail, thousands of others have been reduced to second-class citizenship, defamed, "exiled" internally (as in Russia), deprived of reputation and livelihood, held up to public contumely. This was Stalin's way with the opposition, and it is now ours.'[31]

Stone wrote those words in 1956, in the month that the ironic but effective charge of income-tax evasion was brought against the Communist Party, and the offices of the *Daily Worker* were padlocked. It was eight years after the denunciation of Alger Hiss. The anti-Communist hysteria was prolonged. The Hiss trial for perjury did not end until 1950, when the Red Spy scare revived with the arrest of Julius and Ethel Rosenberg, on charges of masterminding the Soviet espionage network into America's atom-bomb secrets.

The main evidence was the testimony of Ethel's brother, David Greenglass, a spy so amateur that he claimed to have stolen uranium from Los Alamos by putting it in his pocket. Their trial and appeals process was also long drawn-out, and they were finally executed in the electric chair on 19 June 1953. The American mood of the week in which Judge Irving Kaufman passed the first espionage death sentence upon American civilians in peacetime may be recaptured by the front-page headlines of the *New York Times* for 28 March 1951:[32]

ACHESON EXHORTS AMERICANS TO MEET SOVIET PERIL NOW

US POWER MUST 'FRIGHTEN' ENEMY, WILSON ASSERTS

DANGER OF ATOM BOMB ATTACK IS GREATEST IN PERIOD UP TO THIS FALL, EXPERT ASSERTS

RED CHINA REJECTS MACARTHUR'S OFFER

FERRER DENIES HE IS RED

The point that Stone missed, but which was central to Congressman Nixon's design (and he was Vice-President when the Rosenbergs were executed), was not simply to root out and crush the Communists. It was also to intimidate their potential sympathisers among the liberals. As Nixon concluded:[33]

Hiss was clearly the symbol of a considerable number of perfectly loyal citizens whose theaters of operation are the nation's mass media and universities, its scholarly foundations, and its government bureaucracies. They are of a mind-set, as doctrinaire as those on the extreme right,

which makes them singularly vulnerable to the Communist popular
front appeal under the banner of social justice. In the time of the Hiss
case they were 'patsies' for the Communist line.

These arguments carried more force with each year, from the defec-
tion of Igor Gouzenko of the Soviet Embassy in Canada in 1945, with
the first evidence of atom bomb espionage, to Churchill's Iron Curtain
speech the following year. In 1947, the Truman Doctrine and Marshall Plan were predicated on the existence of a death struggle
between freedom and Communism, and in 1948, the Hiss case
suggested that Nixon and Chambers were right, that Communist
moles had indeed burrowed deep inside the American bureaucracy. In
1949 came the final collapse of Chiang Kai-shek and the Communist
victory in China, and the detonation of the first Soviet atom bomb.
And the following year, the divided land of Korea saw dramatic new
evidence that the West's defences might not hold, that the bounds of
containment could fall to armed invasion.

Nixon's sneer at 'patsies' had a particular target, the Secretary of
State, Dean Acheson, who declared that whatever the House Un-
American Activities Committee might say, he 'would not turn [his]
back on Alger Hiss'. For Acheson, this was the code of a gentleman;
for Nixon, the mark of the patsy, soft on Communism. Nixon could
hardly have been more wrong. As Hiss was being convicted, the Policy
Planning group at the State Department were preparing, on Acheson's
orders, the blueprint for the rearming of America and the conduct of
the Cold War. NSC-68, as it was known from its National Security
Council classification, was the considered response of the Truman
Administration to the new threat which followed the fall of China:
'Soviet efforts are now directed toward the domination of the Eura-
sian landmass.'[34]

NSC-68 began with the familiar theme: 'What makes the continuing crisis, is the polarisation which inescapably confronts the slave
society with the free . . . the US must lead in building a successfully
functioning political and economic system in the free world.' The
novelty of the document lay in the cost estimates of this global effort,
raising the US defence budget from its current level of $13.5 billion a
year towards $50 billion. The first drafter, Paul Nitze, had consulted
with Professor Leon Keyserling of the President's Board of Economic
Advisers, to establish that on Keynesian principles of deficit spending,
the US could afford it, and perhaps even benefit from the flood of state-
directed investment. NSC-68 was clear: 'Foreign economic policy is a

major instrument in the conduct of US foreign r
peculiarly appropriate to the Cold War.'[35]

The original plan was to publish the document in a
American and Western opinion. Acheson preferred to k
secret, and to use it 'to so bludgeon the mind of top governm
not only could the President make a decision but that the dec. on
could be carried out'. Kennan loathed the document, which he saw as
crude and mechanistic, and taking the precise lineaments of his own
'containment' theory too far. But NSC-68 pointed out that the
problem of containment was that it required superior military
strength, and now that the Soviet Union had the atom bomb, the US
could no longer afford to bluff its way through with the bomb alone.
Massive conventional rearmament was required, since: 'The Republic
and its citizens, in the ascendancy of their strength, stand in their
deepest peril.'

NSC-68 was certainly aggressive, and in the spring and early
summer, as it circulated around Washington it was seen as out-
landishly expensive. In spite of the support of Pentagon, State Department, CIA and the White House staff, NSC-68 did not entirely
convince President Truman. Indeed, on 1 June, he told a press
conference that the world was 'closer to real peace than at any time in
the last five years'.[36]

Thus three weeks later, the invasion of South Korea on 24 June
came as a complete surprise to Washington, even though a CIA report
of 10 March had predicted an invasion in June.[37] On 20 June, Dean
Rusk, who ran the Far Eastern desk at the State Department, had told
Congress that he saw 'no evidence of war brewing'. And had there
been, all the public pronouncements of US officials agreed that they
would not fight it in Korea. Most US and Soviet troops had been
withdrawn, and spasmodic skirmishes between North and South
Korean troops had become normal enough to be treated with equani-
mity. In March 1949, General MacArthur said that the line of US
defence in the Pacific 'starts from the Philippines and continues
through the Ryukyu archipelago, which includes its main bastion,
Okinawa. Then it bends back through Japan.' On 12 January 1950, in
a speech to the National Press Club in Washington, Acheson repeated
this geographic formula, which carefully excluded the island of
Formosa, the new base of Chiang Kai-shek's exiled government, as
well as Korea.[38]

More to the point, at that press conference Acheson made a
thoughtful and ultimately prophetic argument that Soviet designs on
Manchuria and Sinkiang, and the virtual annexation of Mongolia,

would eventually offend Chinese nationalism. 'Those who proclaim their loyalty to Moscow proclaim loyalty to an enemy of China,' he noted. Either suggestion, that Korea was not inside the American defence perimeter, or that the United States was waiting for an inevitable Sino-Soviet split, might have helped provoke the North Korean invasion. It may also have given Chiang Kai-shek and Syngman Rhee, the South Korean leader who had just suffered a severe setback in his country's election on 30 May, a motive to force the issue and demand US support. The American press noted that after the election, Rhee's regime, which had made repeated threats of invading the North, 'was left tottering by lack of confidence, both in Korea and abroad'.[39]

At a swiftly convened council of war, Truman and his advisers agreed (without consulting their allies) to use US air power against the invading North Korean tanks, and for the first time to give physical protection to Formosa by sending the Seventh Fleet to steam between the island and mainland China. This was not done without trepidation. A Chinese invasion by hordes of wooden junks was expected, and the Seventh Fleet discovered on their first exercise that junks were very hard to sink. 'We didn't have enough shells to fire a single round at each junk,' reported Dean Rusk. None the less, Rusk argued at the war council on 27 June that 'a South Korea absorbed by the Communists would be a dagger pointed at the heart of Japan'.[40]

Truman had one crucial and accidental asset. The Soviet delegates were boycotting the United Nations because the Chiang Kai-shek government still occupied the Chinese seat on the Security Council. Moscow insisted that the seat should go to Mao's government. In spite of Foreign Minister Gromyko's advice, Stalin refused to send back the Soviet delegation to veto any UN action and voice Gromyko's view that: 'The puppet government of South Korea was being egged on by the USA to start war on North Korea.'[41] In the absence of the Soviet veto, and with only Yugoslavia opposed, and Egypt and India abstaining, the UN voted to support South Korea against aggression. Even though there is no doubt that US troops would have fought anyway, they were able to do so under the UN flag. This was something between a fig-leaf and a fiction. General MacArthur later informed the US Senate: 'I had no direct connection with the UN whatsoever.'[42]

There was a grain of truth in Gromyko's argument, but the invasion, and thus the act of aggression, came from the North. Still, there was little sign that the South was prepared or willing to fight for Syngman Rhee's regime. The American troops were willing, but woefully under-equipped. The pace of demobilisation since 1945 had left MacArthur's infantry divisions lacking 62 per cent of their fire-power, and 80 per cent of their sixty-day supply of ammunition was found to be unusable.[43] Within weeks, the US and the remnant of the South Korean forces were driven back and besieged in a small perimeter around the port of Pusan. The demobilisation since 1945 meant that the US had only limited ground forces, and the Pentagon immediately warned against transferring troops from Europe, since the attack on Korea could be a deliberate diversion. But in September, in a daring and amphibious flank attack at Inchon, close to the old border on the 38th parallel, General MacArthur retrieved the situation. His attack used the US Marines, one of the few fully trained and equipped divisions immediately available. Their swift occupation of the capital Seoul, far to the rear of the North Koreans, sent the invaders fleeing back in rout. MacArthur chased them over the border, and all the way up through North Korea to the Chinese frontier on the Yalu River.

What happened next might have been expected. The Chinese had issued enough warnings. 'Crisis, like a volcano, is menacing American imperialism,' Mao had declared at the height of the civil war. 'This situation forced American imperialists to establish a plan for enslaving the world: to plunge like wild beasts into Europe, Asia and other places, muster the reactionary forces of various countries – those dregs spat out by the people – to organise the imperialist, anti-democratic front against all forces headed by the Soviet Union, and prepare war.'[44]

Cables from the Chinese leadership to Stalin in October 1950, recently released from Chinese archives, suggest that Mao's motive in entering the war was essentially defensive. On 2 October Mao cabled: 'If we allow the US to occupy all of Korea, Korean revolution-ary power will suffer a fundamental defeat, and the American invaders will run more rampant, and have negative effects for the entire Far East . . . We must be prepared for the US to declare and enter a state of war with China. We must be prepared that the US may, at a minimum, use its Air Force to bomb major cities and use its Navy to assault the coastal regions.' Mao went on to argue that without a swift victory by the Chinese forces in Korea, leading to a diplomatic settlement, the fate of the Chinese revolution itself was at risk. Such a war, Mao told Stalin, 'would arouse dissatisfaction towards us among the national bourgeoisie and other segments of the people. They are very afraid of war.'

Mao's cable went on to make clear that the Chinese attack depended on the expectation of Soviet help. After the first attacks upon American and South Korean troops inside North Korea 'north of the 38th parallel, they will await the arrival of Soviet weapons'. Although the documentary evidence remains fragmentary, this almost certainly included Soviet air support. Mao's cable says that the attack was planned for 15 October, but Stalin's refusal to deliver the promised military support led Mao to delay the invasion. On 13 October, a second cable from Mao to prime minister Zhou Enlai, then in Moscow to press Stalin for support, said that the Chinese Politburo had unanimously agreed to go ahead with the invasion anyway, and again cited the domestic threat inside China: 'If we do not send troops, allowing the enemy to press to the Yalu border and the arrogance of the reactionaries at home and abroad to grow, this will be disadvantageous to all sides.'

Between those two cables, two US warplanes strafed the Soviet air base at Sukhaya Ryechka, near Vladivostok, sixty miles from the North Korean border, in a surprise attack on 8 October. Eleven days later, ironically the very day Chinese troops began to cross the Yalu into North Korea, the US offered an apology for a navigation error. One of the Soviets who took cover from that raid was General Georgi Lobov, commander of the 303rd air division, who had been transferred in August from the air defence of Moscow to the Siberian front. In 1992, General Lobov for the first time published his own recollection of the strictly limited air war which Stalin authorised him to fight after 1 November 1950. His initial force of 32 MiG-15 jets, later increased to 150, were painted in Chinese colours, the pilots issued with Chinese uniforms and identification papers, and based at the Chinese military airfield of Antung, on the Yalu River. They were not allowed to operate within sixty miles of the battlefront, nor to fly over the sea, and their main role was to defend the Yalu River crossings from American attack. The MiGs came as a sharp surprise to the US and allied aircraft, establishing local air superiority until the US F-86 Sabre jet evened the balance. Some 200 Soviet pilots died in this limited air war, which lasted into 1952, and Lobov claimed that his MiGs shot down at least 1,300 American planes.

Although known to the US Air Force and the US authorities in Washington, the limited Soviet intervention was deliberately kept from the public. Paul Nitze, at the State Department's Policy Planning Staff, prepared a memorandum entitled 'Removing the Fig Leaf from the Hard Core of Soviet Responsibility', but a decision was taken not to release it. 'The argument was that if we publicised the facts, the public would expect us to do something about it, and the last thing we wanted was for the war to spread to a more serious confrontation with the Soviets,' Nitze explained in 1992, when the historian Jon Halliday unearthed this intriguing sub-plot of the Cold War.

China sent diplomatic warnings through India that an invasion of North Korea, or a move to the Yalu, would provoke its intervention. The first Chinese prisoners were taken in October, a full month before the full weight of the Chinese Army intervened to throw the UN forces back far below the 38th parallel. The US troops, and their British and Australian allies (fighting as a Commonwealth division), the Turkish troops and various other national contingents who had rallied to the UN cause, were badly mauled in that terrible winter.

The situation was so desperate that President Truman incautiously suggested to a press conference that the atom bomb might have to be used. This sent Prime Minister Attlee flying across from Britain to seek assurance that the United States would not go nuclear without at least consulting its allies. Truman blithely agreed to do so, until Dean Acheson discreetly reminded him that this would be illegal under US law. An emollient form of words was found which implied, but did not promise, consultation. The military situation was not, in the event, quite so desperate. Finally the UN forces regrouped and with their air power clawed their way back to the original border on the 38th parallel, and established a long and costly stalemate that was to last for another two years, before a truce was signed and the division of the two Koreas became as fixed a symbol as the two Germanies of the world's Cold War partition.[45]

But the real balance of forces around the world had been transformed, far from the battlefield. 'Korea saved us,' Acheson later observed. Without the war, the costly plans of NSC-68 would have faced an arduous uphill campaign. The first defence budget presented by President Truman after the war began was for $50 billion, the precise figure Acheson had hoped for. The US Army doubled, to over three million men. The number of Air Groups doubled to ninety-five, and were deployed to new bases in Britain, Libya, Morocco and Saudi Arabia. Everything changed with Korea. American diplomacy, defence budgets and military reach exploded across the globe in the aftermath of the invasion, as US taxpayers and Congress alike gave the unstinted political support the strategic planners had hitherto sought with only limited success.

The new American activism unlocked a series of diplomatic doors. After months of patient cajoling of the French to accept German economic support in the new Nato, Acheson met the French and British foreign ministers at the Waldorf Hotel in New York and dropped his new bombshell. As the Marines stormed ashore at Inchon, Acheson announced that the US now wanted full-scale German rearmament within Nato, and was prepared to station permanently in Europe four US Army divisions.[46]

Even though a furious row ensued at the Waldorf, as Britain and France and the smaller European allies grasped the enormity of the transformation this implied for America's concept of Germany and for Germany's role in Europe, the French found it difficult to refuse. The month after the Korean War broke out, the Americans decided that the whole of Asia was at risk. Not only had the US sent the Seventh Fleet to guard Formosa, it also agreed for the first time to send a US military mission to support the French in Vietnam. Hitherto, there had been US aid for France, which was understood to be available for use in Vietnam. But now the US commitment to an essentially colonial war had become explicit, against a Vietnamese resistance whose founding document quoted the American Declaration of Independence.[47]

The good fortune of the Soviet walk-out from the UN could never be repeated, so Acheson pushed through a brisk procedural reform of that body which was designed to get around any future Soviet veto. Called 'Uniting for Peace', it gave the General Assembly the right to propose collective security measures, including the use of force, if a Security Council veto blocked urgent action: a cunning ploy when the US dominated the General Assembly, with loyal Latin American votes, but risky in the years after colonial independence during which the General Assembly was flooded with new and independent states.[48]

At the same time, the Korean War transformed the role, the status and the economy of Japan. The classic example is the extraordinary change in the fortunes of Shotaro Kamiya, president of the fledgeling Toyota company. He arrived in the USA on the day the Korean War broke out, desperate to reach a licensing deal with Ford and save his struggling company, then selling barely three hundred trucks a month. He failed; Ford were not interested. When he arrived disconsolately back in Japan, he found it already bustling as the base for the exploding American war effort. Kamiya was greeted by a flood of urgent orders from the Pentagon for 1,500 trucks a month. The profits from the trucks financed Toyota's expansion into passenger cars. After the Korean War, Toyota never looked back.[49]

The Japanese boom was financed by the United States, through a war-emergency system known as Special Procurements. Almost unnoticed at the time, this system pumped $3.5 billion into Japan, which with other US funds meant that Japan received as much as the Marshall

Plan had invested in the West German economy. The Special Procurements were a way for the armed forces to buy supplies locally, without going through the complex purchasing and tender system which the Pentagon was required to follow back in the USA. In 1950, for the first six months of the war, they amounted to $149 million. In 1951, Special Procurements in Japan grew to $592 million. They peaked in 1953 at $809 million, and were still $557 million as late as 1955.[50]

A modern army has a vast hunger for all kinds of supplies, from processed foods to clothing, from oils and lubricants to medical syringes and beer, from paints to disinfectants, bootlaces to matches. Japan supplied them all. The American money went to companies like Toyota for its trucks, to the textile trade for winter clothing, sleeping bags and hospital sheets, and to the health industries for everything from bandages to pharmaceuticals. The investment poured into the muscles of future growth like oil-refining facilities, and to revive the Japanese shipyards. Cargo ships were scarce, and so the United States, which had in 1946 planned to strip the Japanese shipbuilding industry for war reparations, reversed its policy and plunged its Aid Counterpart Funds into new shipbuilding facilities. By 1956, Japan had the most modern shipyards in the world, was launching 26 per cent of the world's shipping, and seizing a lead it was to maintain for a generation.[51]

This change in America's economic policy towards Japan was matched by political shifts. The civil liberties which MacArthur had been keen to introduce in 1945–6 were curtailed with the war. In the month of North Korea's invasion, MacArthur's office ordered the dismissal of seventy Communist Party 'members and sympathisers' from the pro-Communist newspaper *Akahata*. Shortly afterwards, with the US troops reeling back on Pusan, *Akahata* was banned indefinitely, and another 700 Communist sympathisers were purged from the Japanese press. The following year, all the 351 Japanese journalists who had been dismissed in 1945–6 as too sympathetic to the militarist regime of wartime Japan, were reinstated.[52]

Whatever resentments these measures may have inspired were eased by the flood of prosperity. Japan's manufacturing output leapt by almost 50 per cent between March 1950, before the war broke out, and March of the following year. By 1952, Japanese economists estimated that at last living standards had returned to their pre-war levels.[53] And the boom continued. By 1953, manufacturing output was more than twice the level of 1949, with the US war-related funds continuing to pour in to the point where the Japanese recovery became self-sustaining. This was not private investment. Between 1950 and 1966, a meagre total of some $300 million in foreign private

investment came into Japan, less than 9 per cent of the sums that
Special Procurements alone pumped into the Japanese economy
between 1950 and 1955. And all thanks to the American taxpayer.[54]

Not only did the Pentagon, acting on the immediate strategic
priorities of the Korean War, finance the boom which was to create
America's most formidable trade competitor; the US military authorities re-created the management mechanisms which steered Japan to
greater success. Once the Korean invasion began, there was no more
talk of closing or breaking up the zaibatsu. These vast industrial
trusts, institutionally committed to a religion of strategic investments
for long-term growth, were positively encouraged. The beneficiaries
were the three great pre-war zaibatsu: Mitsui (which includes Toyota
and Toshiba and Mitsukoshi department stores); Mitsubishi (which
includes Nikon, Kirin Beer, Meiji Life and NYK Shipping); and
Sumitomo (which includes NEC electronics).[55]

Moreover, they flourished with the help of American management
and production experts who were flown to Japan to teach the most
advanced methods of assembly-line and productivity techniques.[56]
The best-known of these American experts, W. Edwards Deming, the
intellectual father of quality control, is revered in Japan to this day,
where companies compete for the annual Deming Medal.[57] Since the
commercial opportunities of the Korean crisis were obvious to the
Japanese political leaders, they were from the beginning quite explicit
about the relationship they perceived between their prosperity and
their security status under the US occupation.

Prime Minister Shigeri Yoshida, writing in the late autumn of 1950,
with the war under way but before the Chinese counter-attack, spelt
out the bargain in *Foreign Affairs*, the house magazine of the American foreign-policy establishment:[58]

> The UN relief and rehabilitation program will eventually call for
> quantities of building materials, rolling stock and machinery, besides
> clothing and all manner of miscellaneous articles. And we are right on
> the spot to supply them. But in order that Japan may become a real
> workshop of East Asia and contribute abundantly to its progress and
> prosperity, she must have a peace treaty. It is essential that we be
> guaranteed an equitable and equal treatment in international com-
> merce, the rights of travel and residence, and full freedom of trade
> and shipping in this and other quarters of the globe. Such conditions
> of commerce and navigation can be realised only after the conclusion of
> peace and Japan's restoration as a free and independent member of the
> society of nations.

Accordingly, the Japanese peace treaty was concluded in September 1951 by the Republican Senator (later to be Eisenhower's Secretary of State) John Foster Dulles. It returned full sovereignty to Japan's home islands, while granting the US control over the Ryukyu chain, and the main US base of Okinawa. The US also had the right to keep military bases in Japan. Since the country was now more a strategic asset than a defeated foe, the US evidently regretted Article IX, the non-belligerency clause in the Japanese constitution. In 1953, Vice-President Richard Nixon was to describe it as 'an honest mistake'.[59] The clause was popular in Japan, and released government revenues for more productive purposes, but the Japanese Self-Defence Force grew anyway, to 130,000 men by 1954, with a naval arm in 1952, and an air force in 1954.[60]

Japan's prosperity had itself become important to US security, as Dulles explained in discussion meetings of the Council of Foreign Relations while the treaty was being drafted. Since the United States did not want Japan to revive its traditional trading links with now-Communist China, Dulles explained, it was important that those parts of Asia which were not Communist, which included South Korea, South-East Asia, and the countries now known as the Pacific Rim, should remain so. Japan would need access to their raw materials, and their markets.[61] A parallel case was made by Joseph Dodge, the American banker brought to Japan by General MacArthur, in his report *US–Japan Economic Relations in the Post-Treaty Period*. This spoke of 'substantial reliance on Japan . . . for production of goods and services important to the security of the US and the economic stability of non-Communist Asia; cooperation with the US in the development of raw materials resources of Asia; development of Japan's appropriate military forces as a defensive shield and to permit the redeployment of US forces'.[62]

The irony of this was apparently lost upon Dodge and Dulles. America's war in the Pacific had been fought against Japan's 'Greater East Asian Co-Prosperity Sphere'. And now, just five years after winning that war, it had become US policy to help re-establish that sphere. The logic of the Cold War led the USA directly to the deliberate resurrection of Japanese economic power. Once again, the image of the Cold War as tennis match is compelling. America reacted to the 'loss' of China by beginning its reconstruction of Japan. That in turn may have helped inspire the North Korean invasion. And the rhythm of volley and counter-volley went grimly on; the Korean War not only intensified the American resolve to build up Japan, and South Korea and Formosa, as strategic assets, but also inspired the United States to build up West Germany on the far side of the world.

The perilous implications of the Cold War had reconciled France and Britain to the economic revival of West Germany. But they were aghast at Acheson's announcement at the Waldorf Hotel that the post-Korean threat now required German rearmament. France had spent five years under German occupation; Britain had been bombed, blitzed, and impoverished by the exertions of the war against Hitler. Now the Germans were to be not only re-industrialised, but to be restored as a military power. The reaction of the Soviet Union to German rearmament, after its monstrous losses in the Nazi invasion, was inevitably far more strident. It saw American troops and a resurgent Japan on its Siberian front, and once again was faced by German panzer divisions to the west, this time backed up by American industrial might.

The Korean War had not settled very much on the Asian mainland, although the US decision to go to France's support in Vietnam stored up a terrible new harvest for the future. The Korean border remained where it had been, on the 38th parallel. At least 600,000 Koreans died, and close to a million Chinese. Of the United Nations forces, 54,246 Americans died, along with 3,194 of America's allies.[63]

But the Korean War had dramatically sharpened the American purpose, even while giving that purpose a global focus. By going global, the Cold War brought a new intensity, a new Germany, and a new militarisation, back to the heart of Europe. That was not all. For the second time, the US and Soviet Union were learning how to manage the state of crisis between them. The blockade of Berlin had been countered in a way which avoided direct military confrontation. The Korean War, which saw major US casualties and direct clashes between US and Soviet warplanes, was also managed in a way that avoided a wider war. Stalin's limited objective of using the Soviet MiGs to defend the Yalu crossings and sustain the Chinese armies was in effect accepted by the US, and the Korean War ended in an uneasy draw. In Germany, with the Berlin air lift, and in Asia, with the blind eye turned to General Lobov's MiGs, Washington and Moscow alike were learning to operate in a new strategic environment in which the need to prevent a crisis from expanding into full-scale war was more important than any local victory. The Cold War, as a system of international control, was becoming an institution.

Chapter 4

New Leaders and Lost Opportunities

When the horror subsided the floodlights went out
we discovered that we were on a rubbish heap in very strange poses
some with outstretched necks
others with open mouths from which still trickled my native land
still others with fists pressed to eyes
cramped emphatically pathetically taut.

'The Awakening', Zbigniew Herbert

The Cold War had fallen under new management by the time the Korean War armistice was finally signed in July 1953. The three most important governments had been transformed. The first was in Britain, where Winston Churchill's Conservatives won a narrow election victory over Labour and returned to office in October 1951. Four months later, after being embarrassed in the New Hampshire primary election, President Truman decided not to run again for the White House, and General Dwight Eisenhower won the Presidency in November 1952. He did so on an aggressive foreign-policy platform, written by his future Secretary of State John Foster Dulles, which promised not to contain Communism but to confront and to defeat it.

A Republican victory, the party promised, would 'mark the end of the negative, futile and immoral policy of "containment" which abandons countless human beings to a despotism and Godless terrorism which in turn enables the rulers to forge the captives into a weapon for our destruction'. To the alarm of the European allies, Dulles promised a new policy 'to liberate the captive peoples', and to roll back the Soviet and Chinese advance. And while Eisenhower in his election campaign speeches stressed that this liberation would have to be by peaceful means, Dulles pointedly did not.[1]

Six weeks after Eisenhower was sworn in, Joseph Stalin died at his dacha outside Moscow on 5 March, and a period of political uncertainty followed at the Kremlin. The secret police chief Lavrenti Beria was arrested at a Praesidium meeting in June 1953, and Malenkov,

Bulganin, Molotov and Khrushchev organised a loose, collective leadership until Khrushchev used his control of the party machine to consolidate his own supremacy by 1957.

The period of collective leadership introduced a time of extraordinary if tremulous hope. Stalin's death marked an emotional historical moment which gave his successors the opportunity to think and act without his terrifying restraint. Inside the Soviet Union, the writer Ilya Ehrenburg called the period 'the Thaw', in a novel of the same name which condemned Stalin's vaunted 'New Soviet Man' as a self-serving toady.[2] By 1956, Khrushchev had begun opening the gates of Stalin's Gulag, and started a process of *détente* with Yugoslavia, and with the West. The bloody draw in Korea signified not an end to hopes of Soviet and Communist expansion, but an object lesson in the way that even serious conventional conflicts could be kept geographically limited, and prevented from spilling over into the nuclear war which terrified both sides.

The experience of the Korean War offered the possibility of stability, or what Soviet premier Malenkov called 'peaceful coexistence', in a speech to the Supreme Soviet in August 1953, just five months after Stalin's death. Beria had dropped a similar hint even earlier.[3] But this was to be a false stability, at the mercy of events elsewhere. Both sides had reason to believe that, in the long run, their cause must prevail. For the Soviet and the Chinese leaders, the struggle for national liberation from colonial rule in Asia and Africa implied the weakening of Britain and France, and the establishment of friendly new regimes and bridgeheads around a globe which the US Navy and Air Force effectively commanded.

The process of decolonisation, which the Kremlin saw undermining the West from the rear, offered relief from the besetting syndrome of military inferiority which gripped the Soviet leadership. 'I would even say that America was invincible, and the Americans flaunted this fact by sending their planes all over Europe, violating borders and even flying over the territory of the Soviet Union itself,' Khrushchev recalled. 'Right up to his death, Stalin used to tell us, "You'll see, when I'm gone the imperialist powers will wring your necks like chickens."'[4] But as decolonisation gathered pace, there were more and more chickens competing for the West's attentions.

In Iran, the Mossadeq government nationalised Britain's oil holdings in 1951. In Guatemala, the moderately socialist Arbenz government nationalised 400,000 acres of unfarmed banana plantations belonging to the American United Fruit Company in 1952. Arbenz also invited the Communists to join his coalition. In Egypt in the same year, King Farouk's corrupt old regime was shouldered aside in a military coup which eventually brought young Colonel Nasser to power, intent on nationalising the Suez Canal. In Vietnam, the French humiliation at the battle of Dien Bien Phu in 1954 signalled the coming of a new Communist nation.

If the Kremlin hoped that the process of decolonisation would bring them reinforcements and the promise of eventual global victory, the United States and its allies saw their own achievements consolidating healthily in Europe, the heartland of the Cold War. The economic success of the Marshall Plan became plain in Europe even while the Korean War was still being fought. In Western Europe as a whole, industrial production rose by 62 per cent in the two years after the desperately low point of 1947. Such a swift improvement on the previous year's economic figures was reassuring. But the important psycho-logical comparison was with Western Europe's memories of the last years of peace before World War Two. It took until 1951 for Western Europe's food production to increase over that of 1938 by a modest 10 per cent, and industrial production by a far more energetic 43 per cent.[5]

These raw figures of continental growth mask two important developments. The first was that as well as being re-industrialised, Europe was also being rearmed. The European Nato countries increased their spending on defence from $4.4 billion in 1949 to $8 billion in 1951. These were heroic efforts. Britain, for example, increased its defence budget to a straining 18 per cent of GNP in 1951. But they still served to point to the vast disparity in resources between Europe and a USA which had a defence budget of $50 billion in 1951 – six times greater than that of Nato Europe combined.[6]

The second striking feature of the Marshall Plan's contribution to European recovery is the disparity in its impact on various countries. Between 1949 and 1950, West Germany's foreign trade doubled: it rose another 75 per cent the following year. In 1946, the Western zones of Germany had produced 2.5 million tonnes of steel, which soared to 9 million tonnes in 1949, and to 14.5 million tonnes in 1953. The pace of industrial recovery was extraordinary in Germany, dramatic in France, and rather more modest in Britain and Italy.[7]

In France by 1954, industrial production was 50 per cent higher than it had been in the last year before World War Two. The number of tractors on French farms jumped from 25,000 in 1945 to over 100,000 by 1949, the year when France stopped issuing food-rationing coupons. But in Britain, there was far less sign of recovery until September 1949, when the pound was devalued, from $4 to

$2.80 to the pound.[8] The British dollar deficit then began to ease, and to disappear altogether within two years. American Marshall Aid assistance to Britain ended in late 1951, ahead of schedule. But Britain's traditional trading links with its colonies and Dominions had already been eroded by US pressure. At the General Agreement on Tariffs and Trade talks at Geneva, Britain agreed to freeze its system of colonial trading preferences, whose tariffs could henceforth only be reduced, and never raised.[9]

Britain, while by far the strongest military and economic force of the Western European powers, was still locked into the pretensions of not simply great-power status, but of global ambition. A painful decade was to ensue before the Suez débâcle made the country's reduced weight in the world brutally clear. But in the late 1940s and early 1950s, Britain tried to maintain a leadership in Western Europe while simultaneously clinging to the shreds of Empire overseas. Even after the withdrawal from Greece and Palestine and the independence of India, Britain maintained forces around the globe.

In July 1950, when forces had to be found for the Korean War, Britain maintained two infantry divisions and an airborne brigade in the United Kingdom; one infantry and one armoured division in West Germany, with seven more armoured regiments, an artillery regiment and two infantry battalions. There was another infantry brigade in Austria, and two infantry battalions and an anti-tank battalion in Trieste, on the disputed Yugoslav–Italian border. In the Middle East, stretched from Libya through Egypt to the Persian Gulf, there was an infantry division, and three artillery and two armoured regiments. In Malaya, there was a Gurkha division and one infantry and one Commando brigade. And in Hong Kong, there was another infantry division, and an artillery and an armoured regiment. The Royal Air Force maintained 120 squadrons around the globe, and the Royal Navy was still powerful enough to deploy a fleet in the Atlantic, another in the Mediterranean, another in the Indian Ocean, and still send an aircraft-carrier, two cruisers and four escorts to the Korean crisis from the China station.[10]

These were costly forces, betraying commitments beyond Britain's economic strength. And these imperial traditions and post-imperial ambitions inhibited the Labour government from taking the role in Europe which both France and the USA urged upon them. In 1949, as the Marshall Plan worked its magic on the economies and morale of Western Europe, the Americans laid out a vision for the future which was to prove both compelling and defining. The Organisation for European Economic Cooperation, the body which implemented the

Marshall Plan, held a council meeting on 31 October 1949. Paul Hoffman, the president of the Studebaker auto corporation who was the OEEC Administrator, delivered a plan for 'the integration of the European economy'. This was not just an idea, Hoffman insisted, but 'a practical necessity':[11]

> The substance of such integration would be the formation of a single large market within which quantitative restrictions on the movement of goods, monetary barriers to the flow of payments, and eventually all tariffs are permanently swept away. The fact that we have in the US a single market of 150 million consumers has been indispensable to the strength and efficiency of our economy. The creation of a permanent, freely trading area comprising 270 million consumers in Western Europe, would have a multitude of helpful consequences. It would accelerate the development of large-scale, low-cost production industries. It would make the effective use of all resources easier, the stifling of healthy competition more difficult.

Hoffman was spelling out not only the formation of the European Economic Community, but of the target which would not be reached for another four decades, until the EC's maturity in the late 1980s finally brought forth the strategic goal of the European 'single market' by 1992. The main obstacle to Hoffman's ideas was Britain. Knowing of the American support for the idea of an integrated Europe, Bevin wrote to Acheson just before the OEEC conference that while Britain would do everything possible to support the principle, in practice all concerned 'must have regard to the position of the United Kingdom as a power with world-wide responsibilities, as a leading member of the British Commonwealth and sterling area'.[12]

The irony was rich. A large part of the logic to the spread of the British Empire through the Mediterranean and the Suez Canal and the Persian Gulf, around the African shoreline to the Cape of Good Hope, into islands in the Atlantic and Indian Oceans, was to safeguard the sea routes to India, the jewel in the imperial crown. The need for coaling stations as the Royal Navy shifted to steam power reinforced this logic with logistics. Once India became independent in 1947, the strategic case for much of the rest of the Empire began to crumble, and the hard self-interest of commercial calculation came more strongly into play.

Britain's reoccupation of Hong Kong and its hopes of trade with China led her swiftly to recognise Mao's Communist government, even though the United States refused to do so. Britain's dependence on imported oil dictated an aggressive role to secure that oil in Iran and the Middle East, and a pro-Arab tilt to British policies in Palestine which infuriated the American allies. Britain's determination to cling to privileged access to the tin and rubber of Malaya involved its troops in a prolonged and unusually successful guerrilla war. The mineral wealth of South Africa and the copper of Northern Rhodesia reinforced the ties of sentiment, of military alliance and imperial nostalgia.

The British self-interest involved was draped in the concept of the Commonwealth, which had been given legal force by the Statute of Westminster of 1931. This brought together Canada, Australia, New Zealand, South Africa and Ireland as equal and sovereign nations in a free association 'united by a common allegiance to the Crown'. In 1932, under the impact of the Great Depression, this airy concept was given economic force by establishing a system of tariffs, the Commonwealth Preferences. As a way of maintaining the economic advantages of Empire without the political embarrassments, it proved effective and resilient enough to absorb the wave of decolonisation of the 1950s and 1960s. The system finally perished in the 1970s, after Britain joined the EEC.

But the global alternative, which the Commonwealth embodied, prevented Britain from joining wholeheartedly into the cause of European integration which Paul Hoffman had defined, and on which France was to seize. The seduction of the Commonwealth was enduring, lasting far beyond the humiliation of Suez 1956. The Labour Party leader Hugh Gaitskell, influenced by his brother Arthur – who had served in the Sudan civil service – and by socialist leaders in Commonwealth countries like Singapore's Lee Kuan Yew, fought bitterly against joining the EEC at the Labour conference of 1962. It would mean, said Gaitskell, 'selling the Commonwealth down the river . . . the end of a thousand years of history'.[13]

What Britain rejected, France embraced. France adopted the European idea even though her imperial ties and commitments were at the time just as strong as those of Britain, and with a colonial war raging in Indo-China and another about to erupt in North Africa, much more burdensome.[14] The Americans perceived this early, and Dean Acheson was to play off the French and British and also the Germans against one another with considerable skill. 'France and France alone could take the decisive leadership into integrating Western Germany into Western Europe,' Acheson cabled to his lieutenant, assistant Secretary of State, George Perkins, as the Americans prepared for the OEEC meeting.[15] The British may have temporarily prided themselves on a special relationship with the Americans leading to special treatment. The price Britain paid was to exclude themselves from the economic dynamism which European integration entailed, locking them into a pattern of relative economic decline which steadily reduced their value to their American partner.

Just before that OEEC conference at which Hoffman delivered his call for an integrated Europe, America's Ambassadors to the various European countries met in Paris on 21 October. They had to grapple with the emerging reality of alliance politics: that in Britain, France and Germany there were three distinct policies on the future of Europe and the American role within it. The US Ambassadors, including Averell Harriman as Marshall Plan administrator, Chuck Bohlen from the Paris Embassy and George Kennan who intervened by cable from Washington, had all been of similar mind in the simplest stage of the Cold War. It was easy to agree on containment of the Soviet Union; it was far more difficult to agree on the kind of Western Europe best suited to help contain it.[16]

Acheson, backed up by the Pentagon, which saw Britain as strategically indispensable, was prepared to appease Britain's desire to have the financial privileges of European integration without surrendering a scrap of sovereignty or its global role. Kennan blamed matters on the French 'neurosis' about Germany. Bohlen blamed Britain's 'fiction' that it could still act as both a good European and a global power. The Ambassador to Paris (and later to London) David Bruce, complained that Britain's assumption of a special relationship with America, and of an exclusive position in Europe, could upset the whole Europe-wide purpose of the Marshall Plan. Behind these American arguments about Europe lay a series of anguished political debates within the various European countries. The quixotic flavour of national pride and resentment of American power was illustrated by the vote of the French National Assembly, just before the American Ambassadors gathered, 'to prohibit the import, manufacture and sale of Coca-Cola in France, Algeria and the French Colonial Empire'.

The underlying debate was serious and compelling, and dominated the pages of the leading French newspaper of the day, *Le Monde*. The choice was no longer between joining either the Soviet or the American camp. Only French Communists, and not all of them, accepted the thought of a Soviet sphere of influence. The new options, as French recovery got under way, were more subtle. On the one hand lay the Atlantic Alliance with the rich, generous USA, which carried the disadvantages of being non-European and overly pro-British. On the other hand, there beckoned the prospect of a different course, towards a Europe that was culturally Atlanticist, but politically and strategically neutral between the US and Soviet Union. This would be a Europe well enough armed for its own security, and increasingly prosperous through the integration of the various European economies. The leading French historian of the day, Étienne Gilson, argued as follows:[17]

> That which America is disposed to buy from us with their dollars is our blood, once again, in a third invasion of Western Europe which will make the earlier two of 1914 and 1940 look like pleasure parties. It is too much to pay. We have a right to refuse to sacrifice ourselves for the USA. European neutrality is not inconceivable, so long as it is well-armed.

Gilson's arguments, and the support given them by *Le Monde*'s editor, Hubert Beuve-Méry, aroused furious protests, from the French foreign minister Robert Schuman, and from Beuve-Méry's fellow directors of *Le Monde*. René Courtin, the Resistance leader and law professor, and Christian Funck-Brentano, resigned from the board at the end of 1949, writing in farewell: 'If the USA, disheartened by the way in which we thank them for their aid, abandon Europe and France to misery, despair and Bolshevism, then *Le Monde*, Gilson and you will bear some of the responsibility.'[18]

In Britain, the debate was conducted on different terms. There were few voices supporting an embrace of Europe, but many who saw the Commonwealth not only as an alternative to the American alliance, but also, since that alliance looked economically inevitable, as a moderating influence upon it. Even among America's friends, there was a persistent arrogance about the British approach, embodied in one of Bevin's letters to his prime minister, Clement Attlee: 'Now is the time to build up the strength of the free world, morally, economically and militarily with the US, and at the same time to exert sufficient control over the policy of the well-intentioned but inexperienced colossus on whose co-operation our safety depends.'[19]

From left and right throughout the post-war period, the British tone was aggrieved, and sometimes openly resentful of the dependence upon America. From the Conservative Parliamentary benches, Robert Boothby complained at 'selling the British Empire for a packet of cigarettes'. (The US tobacco lobby had insisted that tobacco exports be included in the Marshall Plan, although they were not requested by the Europeans.) From the left, the later Labour leader Michael Foot complained that Britain had become 'a pensioner of America, a junior partner in an American security system'. And in his resignation speech from the cabinet, complaining at the cuts in the National Health

Service to pay for rearmament, Aneurin Bevan charged: 'We have allowed ourselves to fall too far behind the wheels of American diplomacy.'[20]

In Germany, the political debate assumed an acutely political and nationalist form, between the Christian Democrat leader Konrad Adenauer and Kurt Schumacher, the Social Democrat. For Adenauer, an aged Catholic Rhinelander, German unification was a secondary or even lower priority. Instinctively, he thought in terms of the traditional principalities of Bavaria, Prussia, Silesia and the Rhineland which Bismarck had welded into a single national empire just five years before Adenauer's birth. Germany was almost an upstart presence to Adenauer, who spoke repeatedly of the ancient Holy Roman Empire as if it could be reborn in his own day. His first objective for Germany was the restoration of national sovereignty within the western half of Germany. And as he told Dean Acheson at their first meeting in 1949, that sovereignty would probably have to follow his grander vision of Western European integration.

'His great concern was to integrate Germany completely into Western Europe,' Acheson recalled. 'Indeed, he gave this end priority over the reunification of unhappily divided Germany, and could see why her neighbours might look on it as almost a precondition to reunification.'[21]

By contrast, Schumacher wanted a united Germany, and believed that this could be made acceptable to the Soviets if all foreign troops were withdrawn and Germany became formally neutral. This was not an outlandish proposition; in 1954, just such an agreement was reached over Austria. And as early as November 1949, the Soviet Politburo's Georgi Malenkov had suggested in his formal speech on the anniversary of the 1917 Revolution that the Kremlin would support free elections in a unified Germany so long as it was demilitarised and neutral.[22] But for an avowed neutralist, who had lost an arm and a leg in twelve years in Nazi concentration camps, Schumacher spoke in disturbing tones of a traditional German nationalism. He denounced Adenauer as too pro-Western, 'not the Chancellor of Germany but the Chancellor of the Occupation, of the Allies'.[23]

Schumacher's arguments would have been stronger before the crisis of the Berlin airlift foreclosed any serious prospect of Soviet–Western agreement over Germany. 'Our fundamental attitude is to go ahead with the establishment of a Western government come hell or high water,' Acheson told the State Department press corps in May 1949 as the Berlin blockade ended. Against most expectations, Adenauer won the elections of August 1949, and proceeded with a steady pressure towards his goal of full German sovereignty. And just as Japan was to be transformed by America's new strategic priorities of the Korean War, so Adenauer found his way eased by the war on the far side of the globe.

The week before the invasion of South Korea, the American Proconsul in Germany, John McCloy, rejected Adenauer's appeal for a national police force of 25,000 men. The week after the invasion, McCloy accepted it. In the mood of intense panic in Western Germany, so fearful of imminent Soviet invasion that Adenauer's office appealed to McCloy for 200 pistols to defend themselves against Communist fifth columnists, McCloy cabled Washington a dramatic recommendation for German rearmament.

'If no means are held out for Germany to fight in an emergency, my view is that we should probably lose Germany politically as well as militarily without hope of regain. We should also lose, incidentally, a reserve of manpower which may become of great value in event of a real war,' McCloy wrote.[24]

The American decision to seek German rearmament, with Germany as a member of good standing in the Western alliance, was taken in the wake of the Korean invasion. It was not, and could not be, immediately fulfilled. The alarm of France and Britain saw to that. And as the European allies clambered out of that economic prostration which had left them so few options, Washington had to learn to manage the growing complexities of alliance politics. Three main strands of European policy began to emerge. The Germans were keen on the American alliance as the way to recover full sovereignty, and to make the change from occupied enemy to trusted ally. The British supported the United States with distinctive imperial reservations. And the French grudgingly paid lip-service to American tutelage, at least so long as it bought US support for France's colonial wars, while never abandoning the idea of a European third force between the two superpowers.

Ironically, it was the combination and interplay of these three separate policies which created the conditions that gave birth to the European Common Market in the early 1950s, and allowed that Community to prosper and to flourish under an American military umbrella. The EC began with the Treaty of Paris in 1951 as France, West Germany, Italy, Belgium, the Netherlands and Luxembourg formed the European Coal and Steel Community. This arrangement explicitly surrendered their national sovereignty over the production and use of the two key raw materials of industry. Britain refused to join. The Labour government's new foreign secretary, Herbert Morrison, defended this historic and strategic decision in the most parochial of terms, saying: 'It's no good. We can't do it. The Durham miners won't wear it.'[25] In fact, British thinking was far deeper than Morrison's comment would suggest, and was explained in some detail to the one Frenchman who was universally admired in Whitehall, Jean Monnet. The French architect of Europe, who had during the war worked for both the British and French governments, Monnet had drafted Winston Churchill's dramatic appeal for Franco-British union as Hitler's armies conquered Paris in 1940.[26] Monnet wrote after his London talks in 1950:

> Britain has no confidence that France and the other countries of Europe have the ability or even the will effectively to resist a possible Russian invasion. Britain believes that in this conflict continental Europe will be occupied but that she herself, with America, will be able to resist and finally conquer. She therefore does not wish to let her domestic life or the development of her resources be influenced by any views other than her own, and certainly not by continental views.[27]

By staying out, Britain gave France and Germany the room to create and to dominate what became, with the Treaty of Rome in 1957, the European Common Market. But by staying loyal to the American alliance, the Germans and British gave the Common Market the security and strategic breathing space which allowed it to grow. France wanted a policy independent of America; Britain wanted one independent of Europe; and only Germany squared the circle by cleaving steadfastly to the Atlantic Alliance in strategic affairs, while committing Germany's economic future to the emergent Europe. This German commitment in turn helped give the French the prosperity which later allowed de Gaulle to pursue his own vision of neutralist grandeur. In short, the emergence of the EEC was a compromise resulting from three separate national policies of the three leading European powers. It was, like the original decisions to rebuild the economies of the old German and Japanese enemies, an unplanned but fortuitous outcome.

Successive American governments became resigned to the bickerings among their European allies, and there was one very important reason why they had little choice but to do so. Until the 1960s, with the development of the land-based Minuteman and sea-based Polaris intercontinental ballistic missiles, the US nuclear deterrent was dependent on bombers. And until the B-52 intercontinental began to deploy in large numbers in the 1960s, those bombers were B-47s, with a combat range of 1,700 miles, and veteran B-36s, with a combat range of 3,000 miles. Neither bomber could reach the Soviet heartland from US bases. Even with in-flight refuelling, the Strategic Air Command reckoned in 1952 that it required eighty-two bases overseas to be sure of menacing the Soviet Union.[28] During the 1950s, the US nuclear status was uncomfortably dependent upon the airfields of its allies.

To this strategic dependence was added the messianic anti-Communism of the new Secretary of State, John Foster Dulles. Britain and France were encouraged to pursue their distinct national and colonial policies by the Republican Administration which took office in January 1953. The change was dramatic. In 1951, faced with the nationalisation of its only oil supply which did not have to be paid for in dollars, Britain's Labour government had tried and failed to get US support for some traditional gunboat diplomacy against Iran. Dean Acheson, the US Secretary of State, had warned of Soviet intervention, Communist coups in Tehran, disturbances throughout the Middle East, and virtually forced the British to continue fruitless negotiations with Iran.

As soon as Acheson was replaced by Dulles, Britain tried again, in the person of C. M. 'Monty' Woodhouse. A senior official in British intelligence, Woodhouse reckoned that the new Administration would be more amenable. 'The Americans were more likely to work with us if they saw the problem as one of containing Communism rather than restoring the position of the Anglo-Iranian Oil Company,' he explained.[29] So it proved. With the support of Dulles and the CIA, an Anglo-American covert operation succeeded in toppling Mossadeq, and restoring the Shah. The spoils were subsequently divided in accordance with the new realities: Britain's monopoly of Iranian oil concessions was cut to 40 per cent, American companies were given an equal amount, and Royal Dutch Shell and French interests shared the rest.

The Eisenhower Administration was also ready to be of help to its European allies in Indo-China, where the French were going down to defeat in Vietnam. The United States had already supplied the French with $1,200 million in military aid, with US military advisers and with transport aircraft, and in the spring of 1954, serious consideration was given to the use of nuclear weapons. The State Department and Pentagon discussed dropping three tactical nuclear weapons on the Vietminh troops surrounding Dien Bien Phu, and the French foreign minister Georges Bidault later claimed that Dulles had suggested offering US nuclear bombs to France.[30] The final decision not to go nuclear in Asia was taken by Eisenhower himself, after the British allies refused to accede to his plea for 'united action' to contain China.[31] Eisenhower later told his biographer that he had said to his nuclear-minded advisers: 'You must be crazy. We can't use those awful things against Asians for the second time in less than ten years. My God.'[32]

In the event, the Americans and French settled for a compromise on the Korean model, under which Vietnam was partitioned. The Communist Vietminh took the North, and a pro-Western and independent nationalist government took the South. The Vietnamese and their Chinese supporters were put under intense pressure to agree to this settlement at the Geneva peace conference. The French premier, Pierre Mendès-France, threatened to send a million conscripts to Vietnam unless some fig-leaf of an honourable solution was reached. And the American hints of readiness to use the nuclear weapon had not been lost in China.

The Eisenhower Administration had rattled the nuclear sabre before, with equal success, in forcing the Chinese to agree to an armistice in Korea. The US Embassy in Moscow and Pandit Nehru in India were both used to send firm messages to China that the United States was prepared to widen the war unless China and North Korea agreed to a truce. 'The US had already sent the means to the theatre for delivering atomic weapons. This became known to the Chinese through their good intelligence sources and in fact we were not unwilling that they should find out,' Dulles later explained.[33] The nuclear threat was the more credible because it had been made bluntly public in a dramatic foreign-policy statement by Dulles in January 1954, a year after the Eisenhower Administration took office. This Administration was a coalition, of Cold War warriors like Dulles who would go to almost any lengths to challenge the Soviet threat, and of Republican businessmen like Charles Wilson, the former General Motors director who became Secretary of Defense, who feared overstretching the US economy and wanted to curtail the defence budget. For Dulles, the solution was simple: massive retaliation with nuclear weapons would be cheaper than massive conventional forces.

'We need allies and collective security,' Dulles explained in his speech to the Council on Foreign Relations.[34]

> Our purpose is to make these relations more effective, less costly. This can be done by placing more reliance on deterrent power and less dependence on local defensive power . . . Local defence will always be important, but must be reinforced by the further deterrent of massive

retaliatory power. The way to deter aggression is for the free
community to be willing and able to respond vigorously at places
and with means of its own choosing.

This was an alarming strategy not only in itself, but also because the
Pentagon and the growing band of nuclear theorists at the Rand
Corporation in Los Angeles knew it was thoroughly impracticable. It
had taken the Soviet scientists four years to catch up by testing their
first atom bomb. The United States was already working on the next
generation of nuclear weaponry, the hydrogen bomb. The first American test, on 1 November 1952, delivered a twelve-megatonne blast
which removed the tiny Pacific island of Elugelab from the face of the
earth. This time, it took the Soviets just nine months to follow, with
the first Soviet test of a hydrogen bomb, in August 1953. Now the US
no longer enjoyed a thermonuclear monopoly. More alarmingly for
the Pentagon, the US Air Force investigation of the radiation cloud
from the Soviet test discovered the presence of lithium. This suggested
that the Soviets had taken the technological lead. The American H-
bomb required a heavy refrigeration plant, which took its weight to
well over a tonne, too heavy for anything but a heavy bomber to
carry. The lithium in the Soviet device suggested that no refrigeration
was required. Already worried by the vulnerability of its bombers to
Soviet nuclear attack, the US Air Force now had to fear that the Soviets
would be able to mount their much lighter H-bomb on to an intercontinental ballistic missile.[35] The 'missile gap' theory was born and –
suddenly confronted with the prospect of eventual nuclear inferiority
– the United States plunged into development of the Atlas and Polaris
missiles.

At the same time, the nuclear equation was complicated when
Britain exploded her own first atom bomb in October 1952, and
began developing British strategic bombers to deliver this independent deterrent. Partly insurance against being abandoned by the
United States, partly a product of national pride, the British bomb
came at a time of resurgent British confidence about the country's
place in the world. The death of King George VI and the accession of
Queen Elizabeth II provoked an extraordinary sentiment of optimism, touched by atavism. Harking back to the sixteenth-century
days of Good Queen Bess, the new monarch was hailed as the
harbinger of a new Elizabethan age. A series of events contributed to
the patriotic mood. The most popular was the coronation of the new
Queen, happily accompanied by the conquest of Mount Everest by
one of her subjects, the New Zealander, Edmund Hillary. The Fairy

Delta 2 test plane briefly held the world air-speed record. The De Havilland Comet seemed (until it began to crash) to be seizing the potential world market for a jet passenger airliner. Four Oxford University students helped Roger Bannister, the one with the fastest finish, become the first man to run a mile in four minutes. The British economy was recovering quickly, with food rationing progressively abolished until the final item, sweets, was taken off the ration in 1955.

This sense of returning self-confidence was echoed across Europe, but for Britain there were some successes on the diplomatic scene which encouraged a sense of greater grandeur. In Iran, Mossadeq had been toppled and Britain's oil supply was once more secured. Britain was now part of two new regional security systems, modelled rather loosely on Nato: the Baghdad Pact for the Middle East; and the South-East Asia Treaty Organisation, which gave institutional force to Britain's global pretensions. An accommodation had been reached with the new Egyptian government, with agreement to withdraw British troops from the Canal Zone by 1956. The Geneva conference to settle the French war in Vietnam, chaired by Britain and the Soviet Union, suggested both a useful and an independent role in statesmanship. Britain had resisted the US calls for help in Vietnam, and had helped broker an acceptable settlement. Most important of all, the new foreign secretary, Anthony Eden, finally settled the most contentious issue of the Atlantic Alliance, the terms on which France would swallow German rearmament.

Acheson had thought he had resolved it, first in September 1950 in New York, and then again at the Lisbon conference in February 1952. The military price of reassuring the French, by stationing US troops in Europe permanently, had already been paid. But Acheson had been after rather greater game than just German rearmament and the Nato alliance. He had seen the combination of economic integration and a joint defence system leading towards European political integration. Acheson had been encouraged by Jean Monnet, by the Belgian social democrat Paul-Henri Spaak, and by the British. The new Conservative government was, characteristically, all in favour of European integration and a European army, so long as it did not have to include them. As Churchill put it, 'I meant it for them, not for us.'[36]

Acheson had fought a long and successful battle with a suspicious US Senate to authorise the Nato treaty, with its commitment to four US divisions to be based in Europe. He had fought another with the Europeans to gain agreement in principle to the idea of a European Defence Community. This was intended to lead to an integrated defence force that would bring German military manpower, without

German political authority, to the common defence. The vogue word for this process, much favoured by Monnet, was *engrenage*, or enmeshing. The French National Assembly, and the chronically unstable constitutional system of the Fourth Republic, stubbornly refused to mesh, and Acheson left office frustrated.[37]

The EDC had one implacable foe, who was to frustrate America's European policies for years to come, and was honourable enough about his intentions to say so. General Charles de Gaulle, in political exile at Colombey-les-deux-Églises after handing power back to the squabbling civilians, told an interviewer from the *New York Times* that the EDC was 'plain idiocy', and that the idea of integrating the French forces with a German army of up to 500,000 men would never pass the French National Assembly. 'I will do everything against it. I will work with the Communists to block it. I will make a revolution against it. I would rather go with the Russians to stop it.'[38]

With Dulles warning darkly of an 'agonizing reappraisal' of US commitments to Europe, Eden tried again at the London conference of 1954. This time he succeeded, by making the same military commitment that Acheson had already delivered for the Americans. Eden's proposal was that Germany should join Nato as a full member, but pledge never to acquire nuclear weapons. He then went further, and as the French Ambassador wept openly with gratified emotion, pledged to keep four British divisions and a tactical air force on European soil. It was a curious paradox, that to create a credible Nato to defend Europe against the Russians to the East, both Britain and the United States had to commit their forces to the North German plain to reassure the French that a rearmed Germany would not turn its guns once more against its neighbour to the West. The old saw that Nato was a conspiracy to keep the Russians out, the Americans in, and the Germans down was made wellnigh explicit at the London conference. It worked. Germany formally joined Nato in 1955.[39]

Perhaps all this success went to Britain's head. It certainly fed Eden's legendary vanity, and with Churchill's retirement in 1955 Eden finally succeeded to the prime ministership he had so long craved. And France, liberated from the costly war in Indo-China and turning to a similar war to keep its possessions in North Africa, felt confident enough to reassert its traditional position in the Mediterranean. Even with the US Sixth Fleet now the most potent force, that inland sea remained an Anglo-French lake. The British had Gibraltar, Malta and Cyprus as bases. France dominated the northern and southern shorelines. The two powers jointly owned the Suez Canal. And both Britain and France fretted at American tutelage.

A year before the Suez crisis erupted into war, in October 1955, Eden had told his cabinet:

> Our interests in the Middle East are greater than those of the US because of our dependence on Middle East oil, and our experience in the area [is] greater than theirs. We should not therefore allow ourselves to be restricted overmuch by reluctance to act without full American concurrence and support. We should frame our own policy in the light of our interests in the area and get the Americans to support it to the extent we [can] induce them to do so.[40]

The crisis was precipitated by Dulles, who decided in July 1956 to stop the planned American loan to help Egypt build the Aswan Dam on the River Nile. Dulles believed that Egypt's Colonel Nasser was getting uncomfortably close to the Soviet bloc, buying Czech weapons and seeking to undermine the Baghdad Pact. As in Iran, US and British intelligence had been preparing discreet contingency plans to bring down this troublesome Arab leader, and the decision to block financing for the dam was seen by Dulles as a moderate step to bring Nasser to heel. Nasser's response was to seek Soviet financial support and, a week after Dulles's announcement, to nationalise the Suez Canal on 26 July 1956. Assuming US support, or benign indifference, Eden prepared for military action to topple Nasser and maintain Western control of the canal.[41]

With an American Presidential election looming in the autumn, this was not a wise time to assume that the Americans would back what looked like a classic reprise of imperial gunboat policy. Perhaps encouraged by the absence of any reference to the crisis at the Republican or Democratic party conventions of that summer, Eden pressed ahead, calling up British reservists in August. Meanwhile the Egyptians proved just as capable of managing the pilot and control duties of the canal as the Anglo-French company had been.

Even though the US chiefs of staff proposed supporting Britain, on 2 October Dulles warned that Suez was not part of America's obligations to her Nato allies. Dulles went further, stressing that the United States was not 'identifying itself 100 per cent with the so-called colonial powers'. But if America was hesitant, Eden knew that the French were with him, and the French thought that there might be another local ally in Israel. On 16 October, Eden and Selwyn Lloyd, his foreign secretary, travelled to Paris for secret discussions with the French premier Guy Mollet, which were formally agreed in writing on 22 October at another secret meeting at the château of Sèvres, and again on the 24th.

It was a remarkably complex conspiracy. Israel was to invade Egypt through the Sinai, and move on the canal. Under the transparent excuse of protecting an international waterway, British and French troops were then to intervene and occupy the canal. Neither the British cabinet nor the US ally were told of the plot. In conditions of great secrecy, which delayed the arrival of the heavy British armoured forces by slow sea passage, the tripartite adventure began with the Israeli invasion on 29 October. The next day, London and Paris announced their ultimatum to both Egypt and Israel to withdraw from the canal within twelve hours. Israel agreed, in accordance with the plot, and Egypt refused. On 31 October, British warplanes began attacking Egyptian airfields.

Had the British and French ground forces followed hard on the heels of the airstrikes, the plot might have worked. But the slow troop and tank-landing ships were still at sea. The British and French paratroops did not land until 5 November, and by then there had been a hostile American resolution at the United Nations calling for a cease-fire, a Soviet invasion of Hungary, a run on the pound, and an extraordinary phone call to Downing Street from the White House. 'Is that you, Anthony?' it began. 'Well, this is President Eisenhower, and I can only presume you have gone out of your mind.' The call was taken by William Clark, Eden's press secretary.[42] But Eisenhower may have been right about Eden's mental condition. The British prime minister was out of his depth, under intense stress, and gobbling amphetamines.

When Britain and France vetoed the American resolution in the UN Security Council, Dulles reintroduced it in the General Assembly. It was the week of the presidential election, and Eisenhower's campaign speeches were stressing the point: 'We cannot subscribe to one law for the weak, another for the strong; one law for those opposing us, another for those allied with us. There can be only one law, or there shall be no peace.'[43] George Humphrey, the US Treasury Secretary, took the Suez invasion as a personal affront. 'You will not get a dime from the US government if I can stop it, until you have gotten out of Suez,' Humphrey shouted at the British Ambassador. The British Chancellor of the Exchequer, Harold Macmillan, later accused Humphrey of deliberately selling sterling to intensify the run on the pound, which lost 15 per cent of its reserves in November. Humphrey also blocked Britain's perfectly legal application for funds to the IMF.[44]

Worse still, the Soviet Union sent bellicose letters to London and Paris warning of Soviet intervention, and even threatening the use of missiles, unless Britain and France agreed to a cease-fire and to withdraw their troops. The Atlantic Alliance held up well enough for the CIA to pass on the information that this was an empty threat; the Soviets had no such missiles capable of delivering nuclear warheads on London and Paris. But the French took the menace seriously enough to launch their own bid to become a nuclear power.[45]

The logic of this French decision is not clear. Britain was a nuclear power, but this had neither deterred the Soviet threat nor induced the Americans to support its closest ally in an hour of strategic need which was also a deep national humiliation. At the United Nations, only Australia and New Zealand had stood by Britain. Canada had abstained. India had condemned the intervention. West Germany had been appalled: 'Britain and France will face a long, hard, bloody war, while suffering the icy hostility of nations who only yesterday were proud to think of them as friends,' ran the editorial in *Die Welt*.[46]

It was a brutal puncturing of Eden's grandiose dreams of a new Elizabethan age. Even when Eden agreed to the cease-fire and to the troop withdrawal on 6 November, and Eisenhower forgave him over the phone, and invited him to Washington to clear up 'the family spat', the personal links which had so long sustained the Anglo-American relationship suddenly sundered. Eisenhower's aides persuaded him to withdraw the invitation. Perhaps the most frustrating moment of all for the British came when Selwyn Lloyd finally visited Washington, and called on Dulles in hospital, to be greeted with the question, 'Why did you stop?' The answer, of course, was military incompetence. The British had simply not been able to get their troops to Suez fast enough to present the world, and their American ally, with a *fait accompli*.[47]

By cruel contrast, the Soviets had no such logistic difficulties in Hungary. The Soviet motive behind the nuclear threat was to take advantage of Western disarray to distract attention from their own invasion to crush the nationalist uprising in Budapest. This involved two curious ironies. While Britain and France suffered international humiliation from having too little power to enforce their colonial prerogatives at Suez, the Soviets acquired a different kind of international infamy for deploying too much power. And while the Franco-British embarrassment was the result of a thoroughly reactionary policy, the Soviet reassertion of power in Hungary was the result of a bold attempt at the liberalisation of Stalin's empire.

Throughout the Cold War, the purely diplomatic or strategic relations between East and West were always hostage to sudden changes or developments in the domestic politics of each side. Rarely were Soviet and US politics more out of step than in 1953. Stalin's

death and Beria's execution had encouraged the new collective leadership to seek a form of *détente*, just as Dulles came into office with his
policy of roll-back and massive retaliation. The first sign came within
days of Stalin's death, as Zhou Enlai returned from being one of the
pallbearers at Stalin's funeral to break the log-jam over a cease-fire in
Korea. With Moscow's approval, and new promises of Soviet economic support, he reversed the Chinese insistence that all Chinese and
North Korean prisoners be repatriated.[48]

In an attempt to comprehend what was now facing them, the
Central Committee commissioned the private translation of the available American documentation. Georgi Arbatov, later director of
Moscow's USA and Canada Institute, was assigned James Burnham's
Containment or Liberation in 1953. The Russians were right to be
baffled. Dulles was saying one thing, but on 16 April, a month after
Stalin's death, President Eisenhower was saying another. In his speech
to the American Association of Editors, Eisenhower held out the
prospect of normalising relations now that Stalin had gone.

The Soviet bewilderment was plain. *Izvestiya*, the official journal of
the Supreme Soviet, which was Malenkov's power base, reprinted the
speech in full; *Pravda*, official journal of the Central Committee, and
thus under Khrushchev's influence, published a critical comment-
ary.[49] Then the author of the 'Iron Curtain' speech confused Moscow
further. In May, Winston Churchill spoke of the possibility of a
'spontaneous and healthy evolution which may be taking place inside
Russia', and proposed in the House of Commons a summit meeting
between himself, Eisenhower, and Malenkov. Eisenhower rejected the
idea.[50]

The confusion of the Moscow collective leadership became intense
over Berlin. In May, the East German government announced that it
had been over-hasty in collectivising agriculture and retail trade and
promised relaxation. The Soviet contribution to this gentle thaw was
to remove political authority from the Soviet military commander,
and shift it to a civilian Commissioner. This commissioner in turn was
charged with 'maintaining relations with the occupation authorities
of the US, Britain and France in all questions of an all-German
character'.[51] This sounded as if Moscow were trying to turn back the
clock to the joint-control system in force before the Berlin airlift. But
then in June, the East German government suddenly raised the factory
production targets which were linked to wages. This effective cut in
incomes provoked demonstrations, which turned into riots, that
became a general strike, cheered on by the US radio stations in West
Berlin. Soviet tanks were deployed in East Berlin, Leipzig, Dresden

and Jena. There was shooting, and a still unknown number of deaths, and the CIA station chief in Berlin, Henry Heckscher, cabled back for permission to arm the Berlin workers with sub-machine-guns.[52] He was refused. Dulles's vaunted policy of 'roll-back' proved hollow when tested.

But a form of Soviet roll-back, a voluntary withdrawal of military forces from advanced strategic positions, had begun long before Dulles came to office. The Red Army had withdrawn from eastern Czechoslovakia in December 1945, in parallel with the US withdrawal from the western half of the country. In the spring of 1946, Soviet troops withdrew from northern Iran, and from the Danish island of Bornholm with its strategic position in the Baltic, and from Manchuria. The Soviet army was reduced to 2.8 million men under arms by the outbreak of the Korean War in 1950. The image in Dulles's mind of a relentless Communist advance looked very different from Moscow's perspective. But just as the Korean War had led the US to strengthen its alliances and rebuild its former adversaries in Europe and Asia, the Soviet system reacted in a broadly similar way. The Red Army grew back to 5.8 million men by 1955, even while Malenkov was making speeches about the need for 'peaceful coexistence', and the Soviet army was withdrawing from its zone in Austria and from the Finnish naval base of Porkkala.[53]

Both Moscow and Washington had reason to be confused by the difference between what the other superpower was doing and what it was saying. In each case, internal politics had much to do with this. The difference in the way *Izvestiya* and *Pravda* reacted to the Eisenhower speech of April 1953 reflected the emerging rivalry between Malenkov and Khrushchev. This was not only played out in the sphere of foreign policy, but in domestic planning, with Malenkov pressing for more investment in consumer goods, and Khrushchev wooing the armed forces by stressing the need for more heavy industry and modernised defence production. Khrushchev also won the support of Molotov by agreeing to tighten the security coordination with the Eastern European countries through what became the Warsaw Pact. Malenkov argued that nuclear weapons made peaceful coexistence 'both necessary and possible'. Khrushchev countered that the proletariat was not to be cowed by the nuclear threat, when the vastness of the Soviet Union and the smaller size of its cities left it less vulnerable than the US.[54]

When Malenkov was forced to resign in February 1955, the prevalent Western reaction was that Khrushchev, the hard-liner, had triumphed.[55] This proved to be unfounded. Khrushchev's priority was to repair the damage Stalin had done within the Soviet camp. In 1954, he made a formal visit to China for the ceremonial return of Port Arthur to Chinese control, and to announce closer economic links, agreeing to send Soviet technical experts to build 150 strategic industrial centres. Khrushchev then set about repairing the rifts Stalin had made on the western frontier, flying to see Tito in Belgrade. He delivered a formal apology, and withdrew Stalin's otiose definition of the Tito government as 'a military Fascist dictatorship'.

Stalin's death provided a perfect excuse for the new course at home and abroad. It was easy to blame everything on the old dictator. In May 1955, Khrushchev overrode Molotov's objections to the Treaty which guaranteed Austrian neutrality, withdrew Soviet troops, and them demanded in return a summit.[56] This was a considerable Soviet concession since in the same month West Germany was formally granted full sovereignty, Nato membership, and the right to rearm. Although inevitable, this represented a major defeat for Soviet German policies since 1945. Accordingly, the Warsaw Pact was formally signed as a military counterweight to Nato in the same month.

Dulles was deeply suspicious of Khrushchev, warning the American people in a radio broadcast that 'the new set of dangers comes from the fact that the wolf has put on a new set of sheep's clothing, and while it is better to have sheep's clothing on than a bear's clothing on, because sheep don't have claws, I think their policy remains the same'. But the Geneva summit took place, with Britain, France, the United States and the Soviet Union all attending. Although the Russians bizarrely suggested that if Nato was indeed dedicated to peace, then the Soviet Union might be permitted to join, very little was decided. After asking Gromyko whether he was indeed serious, Dulles agreed to consider the application, and nothing more was ever heard of the matter. 'They simply hushed it up,' Gromyko later complained. The main achievement of Geneva was the very fact that the session took place, the first summit since Potsdam, and the first serious sign of relaxed tension since the Berlin crisis. For months thereafter, *Pravda* referred to 'the spirit of Geneva', so at least it helped Khrushchev persuade his home audience that he had engineered a more hopeful international outlook than Stalin.[57]

The price of this relaxation was the quasi-permanent division of Germany, much to the horror of West German Social Democrats and conservatives alike. Axel Springer, the newspaper magnate, flew to Moscow to inquire whether it was still possible to have unification in return for neutrality. His flagship newspaper, *Die Welt*, stressed: 'Only one way is open, to co-exist with Russia by moving a nonaligned, independent state.'[58] But that option had been overtaken by events. Ever the pragmatist, Khrushchev accepted the new situation in Germany, opening formal diplomatic relations with the Adenauer government in September 1955, and granting East Germany sovereignty over its own foreign affairs at the same time.

The high point of Khrushchev's thaw came early in the following year, with the twentieth Congress of the Communist Party and the celebrated secret speech which for the first time condemned Stalin's crimes from the party's own inner sanctum. The purge of Beria had forced the first round of releases from the Gulag. Some ten thousand political prisoners were freed by 1955, and the great flood of millions of releases came after Khrushchev's speech in the following year.[59] The denunciations of Stalin's terror in the secret speech, deliberately leaked to a Western correspondent through the former KGB official Kostya Orlov, has overshadowed the rest of the proceedings of the twentieth Party Congress.[60] But Khrushchev's open remarks on foreign policy were almost equally significant.

Khrushchev simply ditched the classic thesis of Marxism–Leninism that capitalism and imperialism made war inevitable. That had been true before 'the world camp of socialism became a mighty force', he said. 'At the present time, however, the situation has changed radically . . . War is not fatalistically inevitable.' He went on to acknowledge that there were different forms of transition from capitalism to socialism, including the parliamentary route of free elections which 'may become an organ of genuine democracy'. The socialist camp would win eventually, he insisted, because 'the socialist mode of production possesses decisive advantages over the capitalist mode'. But this did not mean the Soviet Union was seeking to export revolution – 'it is ridiculous to think that revolutions are made to order'.[61]

The implications of Khrushchev's public and private speeches reinforced one another with devastating effect. On the one hand Stalin's authoritarian way was discredited, and on the other the methods of parliamentary democracy were hailed. For the authoritarian Chinese party, this was a shock; for the countries of Eastern Europe, it was something close to a promise of liberation. The dissolution in April 1956 of the Cominform, Stalin's chosen vehicle for the enforcement of orthodoxy, added to the rising expectations. So did the removal of Molotov from his post as foreign minister. And so did Khrushchev's new readiness to make Moscow far more open to the world, welcoming the new leaders of the newly independent

states, and travelling himself to China and India, to Britain and
France.

Khrushchev visibly enjoyed himself in this flurry of public diplomacy. And the rapturous reception he received in India, where he and
Bulganin had to be rescued and lifted by their escorts above the heads
of the enthusiastic crowds, became a propaganda victory in itself.
This was clearly not the grim Stalinist style. Khrushchev was open to
the world at a time when the world itself was opening, and Khrushchev's Moscow seemed far more in tune with the emerging Third
World than did America and its Western allies, still fighting their
rearguard battles for the remaining colonies.

The Bandung conference of Asian and African states in April 1955
represented the moment when this Third World tried to come of
political age, and to define some room for independent manoeuvre
between the two blocs. This was not easy, with pro-American Japan
attending, alongside Communist China, while India's Pandit Nehru
tried to define what national sovereignty and underdeveloped solidarity could mean in a Cold War world. China announced, and the Soviet
Union later supported, the Five Principles of Co-Existence, which were
offered as a code of conduct for world affairs. Originally presented to
India by Zhou Enlai, they proved of little value when China and India
went to war five years later over a territorial dispute in the Himalayas.
The Five Principles pledged mutual respect for each other's territorial
integrity and sovereignty, non-interference in each other's internal
affairs, non-aggression, equal and mutual benefits in economic relations, and peaceful coexistence.[62]

The elevated language of the Five Principles contained one carefully
placed booby trap for the West, or at least for its investors, banks and
developers, whether public or private. Equal and mutual benefits in
economic relations was something that capitalist economies, by definition, found difficult to manage. Unless given in the form of grants or
soft loans with non-market interest rates, Western aid and investment
sought a profit. This also applied to the World Bank and International
Monetary Fund. The Soviet Union, by contrast, was able to point to
the generosity of its economic support for China, for India, and
subsequently for Egypt. Bandung was the moment when this implicit
economic rivalry between West and East took on a strategic dimen-
sion, as the countries of the developing world ceased to be pawns and
spectators in the global rivalry, but began to become players in their
own right. Egypt's Colonel Nasser took advantage of the meeting
with Zhou Enlai to ask him if China or the Soviet Union would supply
the arms the United States had failed to deliver, and also whether the

Soviet Union might help finance the Aswan Dam. When Dulles tried to pressure Nasser by withdrawing the Aswan finance, Nasser already had his alternative, thanks to Bandung.[63]

Bandung and the Geneva summit of 1955 emphasised Khrushchev's success in convincing both First and Third Worlds that the Soviet Union was under new and rather more promising management. Khrushchev's speech at the twentieth Party Congress of 1956 convinced the Second, or socialist World too. And that, ironically, was to prove the trouble. As Mikhail Gorbachev was to learn a generation later, Soviet leaders may unleash change and stimulate expectations; the trick is to control them. And in Eastern Europe, they began to get out of control very fast. Within a month of Khrushchev's speech, the Polish party leader Bolesav Bierut died of what seems to have been natural causes. The Polish party wanted to replace him with Roman Zambrowski, quickly vetoed by Moscow apparently because of his Jewish origins.[64] Edward Ochab took over, presumed loyal by Moscow because of the venom with which he had denounced the purged Polish 'Tito-ist' Wadisaw Gomuka.

Gomuka had been one of those Eastern European Communists who had believed sincerely in the possibility of a different, national form of socialism in the wake of World War Two. General Secretary of the Polish party until the Cold War turned icy, Gomuka had said publicly in 1948 that Tito and the Yugoslav Communists should have been conciliated rather than condemned. When Stalin reasserted complete party control from Moscow, Gomuka was dismissed, expelled from the party, and finally imprisoned in 1951. Released after Stalin's death, as part of the wave of hesitant relaxation which freed an entire generation of Stalin's victims in Eastern Europe, Gomuka was a national symbol.

So when the new Polish government of Ochab began to liberalise in 1956, and came under instant pressure as the workers of Poznań began to strike for more, Gomuka represented a form of Communism that both Polish strikers and Moscow might be prepared to swallow. Ochab's government had little choice. The strikes were serious, and on what was to become known as Black Thursday, Ochab sent two divisions and 300 tanks of the Polish Army to suppress their own people. Most estimates reckon that at least a hundred Polish workers were killed, and another three hundred wounded. Gomuka summed up the result: 'The loss of the confidence of the working class means the loss of the moral basis of power.'[65]

Bulganin and Marshal Zhukov flew in from Moscow for the Polish party's emergency plenum of the Central Committee, insisting that the Poznań strikes and riots be blamed on 'imperialist agitators'. They also declared that Gomuka would not be an acceptable member of any reformed Polish government. Ochab stressed that there was little choice, and won Chinese support for the right of the Poles to resolve their own problem at the eighth Congress of the Chinese Party in Beijing in September.[66] Khrushchev was torn between his unwillingness to return to Stalin's ruthless domination of Eastern Europe, and the pressure from the hard-liners in Moscow to crush this threatening development. The Chinese reaction may have proved decisive.

Khrushchev flew unexpectedly to Poland for another emergency plenum in October, so unexpectedly that his aircraft was bounced by Polish fighters until belated clearance was received from Warsaw.[67] This may have explained Khrushchev's furious waving of his fist at the Polish party leaders who gathered to meet him, and the sudden deployment of the Soviet troops in Poland into positions from which they could attack the cities. But it may also have persuaded Khrushchev to take Gomuka seriously when he warned that if the Soviet troops attacked, the Polish Army would fight back, and he would rouse the Polish people against the invader.

Once he assessed the mood of the Polish party, and heard of the mushrooming of workers' councils, and the meetings of peasants declaring the end of their hated collective farms, Khrushchev grumpily accepted Gomuka as the new General Secretary. When he was assured that Poland would continue to be a firm ally of the Soviet Union and remain within the Warsaw Pact, Khrushchev also swallowed the removal of Marshal Konstantin Rokossovsky as head of the Polish armed forces. Khrushchev's options were limited. As Gomuka said in his address to the plenum, the events in Poland were a direct result of Khrushchev's own speech to the twentieth Party Congress in Moscow. In accordance with that speech, Gomuka went on, he now intended to pursue 'the Polish path to socialism'.

Khrushchev could accept that, and accept the immediate release of the Roman Catholic Cardinal Stepan Wyszynski, so long as Poland remained loyal in the strategic sense. And indeed, the cardinal swiftly reached a concordat with Gomuka which pledged that 'the State would find in the Church hierarchy and clergy full understanding'.[68] But already the wave had spread beyond Poland, and the day that Gomuka told a mass meeting of 500,000 people in Warsaw that the Soviet troops were returning to their bases, the students of Budapest began their own demonstrations. When the Hungarian police moved against the students, the Budapest workers joined them, and together they toppled the giant statue of Stalin in the Hungarian capital.

In panic, Moscow and the Hungarian party looked for Budapest's version of Gomuka, an acceptably nationalist Communist, preferably one who had served a prison term in Stalin's day. Imre Nagy, the former prime minister, who had been purged but not arrested, did not quite fit the bill. But in the sudden collapse of party and government authority in Budapest on the night of 23–4 October, the Hungarian Central Committee could come up with no one better. By the time he took office as prime minister the next day, Soviet T-34 tanks were already rumbling into Budapest. They were greeted with Molotov cocktails and barrels of liquid soap which made their tracks spin helplessly on street corners. The CIA broadcasting network, Radio Free Europe, reported it all breathlessly, and constantly declared the West's solidarity with the Hungarian freedom-fighters.[69] Thus encouraged, and with the support of elements of the Hungarian Army, the Budapest rebels began looting party buildings, and the Hungarian secret police were hunted down like rats in their own dungeons.

Nagy announced an amnesty for political prisoners, and invited non-Communists into his government. He assured Moscow of Hungary's loyalty, and in the hope of a Hungarian version of Gomuka's national-Communism, Khrushchev withdrew Soviet troops from Budapest on 28 October. They were still pulling out when the long-delayed Suez conspiracy was triggered, and Israel invaded the Sinai peninsula. American attention was torn between two crises, and their own imminent Presidential election. Radio Free Europe continued to give an encouragement which proved hollow, and Yuri Andropov, the Soviet Ambassador, looked desperately for someone more reliable than the weak and vacillating Nagy.

In Janos Kadar, who had served a prison term in Stalin's day for 'nationalist deviationism', Andropov found his man, and the basis for a deal. On 30 October, the terms were spelt out, with a formal Kremlin statement of principle on the future relations between socialist states.[70] In effect, it said that loyalty to the Warsaw Pact would guarantee non-interference by the Soviet Union in the internal affairs of allied countries. Perhaps encouraged by Radio Free Europe, certainly under pressure from the growing confidence of his own nationalist supporters, and doubtless carried away by the sheer pace of events, Nagy replied the same day. Hungary was leaving the Warsaw Pact, announced its neutrality, and appealed to the United Nations for support.

This was too much. Khrushchev began a round of consultations, with the Chinese deputy leader Liyu Shaoqi who was visiting Moscow, with Gomuka at Brest-Litovsk, with the Czech and Romanian leadership in Bucharest and even with Tito on the island of Brioni. They all agreed: Nagy had gone too far.[71] On 4 November, as the lumbering British troopships ploughed towards Suez and the British and French paratroops boarded their aircraft, 200,000 troops and 2,500 tanks of the Soviet Army stormed back into Budapest. First reports claimed that at least 20,000 Hungarians lost their lives. In fact, the final death toll was around 3,000.[72]

In Washington, President Eisenhower's staff were checking the last election-eve speeches, in order, as one of them put it, 'to tone down Dulles's references to "irresistible" forces of "liberation" unleashed in Eastern Europe'. In Eisenhower's own speech was a plaintive promise to Moscow 'to remove any false fears that we would look upon new governments as potential military allies'. Once the speech was delivered, and the die cast, the President turned to Emmett John Hughes and spoke of his fears of Moscow:[73]

> Those boys are both furious and scared. Just as with Hitler, that makes for the most dangerous possible state of mind. And we better be damn sure that every Intelligence point and every outpost of our armed forces is absolutely right on their toes. And if these fellows start something, we may have to hit 'em — and if necessary, with everything in the bucket.

The West did not stir. The last plaintive appeals of Radio Budapest for American help gave way to curses and accusations of betrayal before the airwaves fell hauntingly silent. Refugees mobbed the Austrian frontier as Janos Kadar began his national-Communist government. In Italy, the old socialist leader Pietro Nenni, who had in 1948 split his party rather than abandon his alliance with his wartime comrades in the partisans, finally broke with Communists in disgust. Nenni even sent back the money he had been awarded with his Stalin Peace Prize, and took his Italian socialists into a coalition government with the Christian Democrats he had spurned.[74]

The Communist parties of the West, already reeling under the revelations of the secret speech, plumbed the depths of shame. Far away in Ohio, the veteran American Communist John Steuben, a union man who had spent his life among the steelworkers of Cleveland, was dying. He had always been loyal to Moscow, through Stalin's Terror, through the purges, through the Nazi–Soviet Pact and the vilifications of Tito. He had endured, through the beatings by the anti-union goon squads of the 1930s and through McCarthy's witch-hunts, because it was part of his larger loyalty to the cause of the working class, and the ideals of Communism. But the bloody repression of Hungary proved too much, and with his last words, he spoke for many like him: 'I want to live the rest of my life in agony and silence.'[75]

Chapter 5

Spies in the Sky: Sputnik to U-2

The capitals are rocked with thunder
Of Orators in wordy feuds.
But in the depths of Russia yonder,
An age-old silence broods.

'Russia', Nikolai Nekrasov

'We accuse the Soviet Government of murder,' said the editorial in the *New York Times*, as the blood dried on the tank tracks in Budapest. 'We accuse it of the foulest treachery and basest deceit known to man. We accuse it of having committed so monstrous a crime against the Hungarian people yesterday that its infamy can never be forgiven or forgotten.'[1]

Within three years of that denunciation, Nikita Khrushchev was being honoured and fêted on the first visit to the United States by a Soviet leader. But by then, one of the more unexpected results of the bloody suppression of Budapest was starting to become apparent. In Gomuka's Poland, as in Tito's Yugoslavia and even in Kadar's Hungary, that national-Communism which had been hesitantly tried ten years earlier was given a deliberate chance to show that it might work. The curious result of the Soviet brutality in Hungary was that it produced rather more tolerable regimes in Poland and Hungary than those countries had suffered before the uprisings.

But first the whip was cracked, with trials and executions in Hungary. Promises of safe passage for negotiations were made to Imre Nagy and to the leaders of the Workers' Council who had called a general strike, only to be broken. They were arrested and Nagy was later shot. On 15 January 1957, the Kadar government enacted the death penalty for any workers who went on strike in key industries.[2]

Some strikingly independent new shoots flourished in this period, from Leszek Kolakowski's deeply moralistic attempt in Poland to define a liberal Marxism, to the Yugoslav party's defence of the rights to private property and its denunciation of 'every aspect of ideological monopoly'. Doubtless in some shame, and certainly in some fear of unrest spreading throughout Eastern Europe, Gomułka and later Kadar were given significant economic concessions. The equivalent of $500 million in Polish 'debt' to the USSR was cancelled, new trade credits were offered. Polish citizens living in the USSR since 1940 were allowed to return home. The need to buy off Eastern European unrest was to cost Moscow the rouble equivalent of $1 billion in 1957. This sharply reduced the aid available for China, with what were to prove momentous results.[3]

The Soviet Union of the 1950s could easily afford the sudden flood of aid to the Warsaw Pact nations. It was enjoying an economic boom. From 1950 to 1958, the Soviet Union claimed an annual 7.1 per cent growth in its gross national product, more than half as large again as the US rate.[4] The year after Stalin died, the state prices paid for agricultural products were raised, the collective farms were to be paid extra for any food they produced above their quotas, and the tax on the peasants' private plots was halved. In 1958, the taxes were scrapped altogether.

The results were remarkable. By the 1960s, these private plots, which amounted to less than three per cent of the arable land, were producing over thirty per cent of the country's fruit and vegetables. Old-age pensions were increased in 1956, the working week was cut. Industrial production rose that year, so the official statistics said, by 11 per cent. The Virgin Lands, the traditional pasture lands of northern Kazakhstan put under the plough for the first time, began to produce and that year saw a record harvest of 127 million tonnes. The Lenin stadium, the world's largest sports complex, was opened in Moscow, and the first nuclear-powered ship, the icebreaker *Lenin*, was launched the next year.

The symbols of relaxation, most haunting in the return of the 'Zeks' from Stalin's not entirely emptied Gulag, were everywhere. The Kremlin, closed to all but the party élite in Stalin's day, was opened to the public, and on New Year's Eve there was a party for the children of Moscow. There were visas for Western tourists, and an international youth festival which brought rock 'n' roll to Moscow, and left behind two subterranean youth cults, the *shtatniki* (America-lovers) and the *beatniki*. Such was the enthusiasm for Western popular music that a lively cottage industry grew up, and since there was no vinyl, depended on used X-ray film to make bootleg records. A new generation of young poets began declaiming unorthodox verse in Pushkin and Mayakovsky squares. And Alexander Solzhenitsyn, among millions of others freed from the camps, began to write.[5]

Barely noticed in the West, or dismissed as so much propaganda after the slaughter in Budapest, the changes within the Soviet Union suddenly thrust themselves upon the world's attention on 4 October 1957 as the first man-made satellite was launched into space. The Sputnik (the word means fellow-traveller), with its cheeky electronic beeps, was announced as a Soviet contribution to the UN's world geophysical year. The proven capacity to launch a 184lb payload in space orbit was not interpreted as a peaceful gesture by the West, which belatedly remembered Khrushchev's earlier and disregarded claim that the Soviet Union had developed the world's first inter-continental ballistic missile. The implicit threat was clear. The American homeland was now in pawn to superior Soviet technology.

'America has lost a battle more important and greater than Pearl Harbor,' Dr Edward Teller, the father of the American H-bomb, told the national TV audience. 'The Russians have left the earth and the race for control of the universe has started,' commented Senator Lyndon Johnson's adviser, George Reedy. The *New York Times* reported that, on its first day in space, the Sputnik had been 'tracked in four crossings over the US'. In the White House, the shock was visceral. James Killian, appointed by President Eisenhower to be his scientific adviser, later recalled, 'What I felt most keenly was the affront to my national pride.'[6]

The beeps of Sputnik, followed a month later by the launch of a larger satellite which contained a small dog called Laika, echoed in the ears of a top-secret US committee which was composing an alarming document known as the Gaither Report. They delivered its twenty-nine pages, officially entitled *Deterrence and Survival in the Nuclear Age*, to the President on 7 November. One month later, on the anniversary of Pearl Harbor, the United States tried to launch its counter, a tiny 4lb satellite aboard a Vanguard rocket. It rose just twenty-five inches from the Cape Canaveral launch pad, before falling back in full view of the world's waiting news cameras. The contrast could hardly have been more humiliating. London's *Daily Mirror* summed up the disaster with a front-page headline that paid a wry tribute to both Soviet achievement and American failure – 'Phutnik'.[7]

Worse was to come. Just five days before Christmas, the *Washington Post* published an account of the secret Gaither Report, and in sensational language rammed home the frightening implications as explained to the President by America's strategic experts:[8]

> The still top-secret Gaither Report portrays a United States in the gravest danger in its history.

It pictures the nation moving in frightening course to the status of a second-class power.

It shows an America exposed to an almost immediate threat from the missile-bristling Soviet Union.

It finds America's long-term prospect one of cataclysmic peril in the face of rocketing Soviet military might and of a powerful, growing Soviet economy and technology which will bring new political, propaganda and psychological assaults on freedom all around the globe . . .

Only through an all-out effort, the report says, can the US hope to close the current missile gap and to counter the world-wide Communist offensive in many fields and in many lands.

This was not quite the tone of the report, but the *Washington Post*'s spine-chilling version set the mood for the wave of something close to national panic which followed. The report proposed a crash investment on $20 billion in nuclear fallout shelters, and so school districts around the USA began staging air-raid warnings in response to the demands of local parents and politicians. Private enterprise rose to the challenge, with a family-size fibreglass-and-concrete shelter for $2,395, installation extra.[9]

The missile gap implied a technological gap, which in turn implied a research gap, and thus an education gap and so on. In the space of three months, the United States had passed from a blithe self-confidence in its security, its economy and its technology and plunged into a form of national inferiority complex. There were other roots of the insecurity; another Presidential illness, with Eisenhower's stroke in the month after Sputnik was launched, and also the first harbinger of what was to prove a debilitating and shaming confrontation with the unsettled tragedy of America's racial heritage. That summer, the governor of the southern state of Arkansas, Orval Faubus, had sent his National Guard into the city of Little Rock to prevent the racial desegregation of its schools. Eisenhower eventually, after deep hesitation, sent US paratroopers of the 101st Airborne into the city to enforce the desegregation law, and prevent the ugly mobs from intimidating black children. This was not in any sense an American Budapest, but like the Anglo-French invasion of Suez, it served to blur the moral lesson of Hungary. And Eisenhower's White House knew it.

'The crude practice of racism in the self-styled sanctuary of freedom,' sighed Eisenhower's speechwriter, Emmett John Hughes.[10]

The tale carried faster than drum signals across black Africa. It summoned cold gleams of recognition to the eyes of Asians, quick to

see the signs, in the heartland of America, of the racial enmities that had
helped to make colonialism through the generations so odious to them
. . . to all peoples, in all lands, the trained and instructed voice of Soviet
propaganda could relay, in almost affectionately fastidious detail, the
news of Little Rock.

One of the great merits of Eisenhower, stemming from an almost
unparalleled experience of war and crisis, was that he very seldom
panicked. He did not do so now. The Gaither Report warned that the
Soviet economy was growing with dramatic speed; that their
machine-tool industry was out-producing that of America; that the
United States faced an increasing threat which might become critical in
1959 or early 1960; that they had produced the fissile material for
1,500 nuclear warheads, and that in missile technology 'they have
probably surpassed us'. It recommended increasing the US defence
budget by 50 per cent forthwith. Hard on Gaither's heels came the
new mandarins of nuclear theory from the Rand Corporation, telling
a stunned White House briefing that under the current alert and
warning system, the bombers of Strategic Air Command could be
destroyed in a Soviet surprise attack. The United States had no
guaranteed retaliatory force; it thus had no credible deterrent.[11]

Eisenhower did not swallow it. He knew from intelligence reports
that the Soviet missile production capacity for the new Semyorka
ICBM was low, and that the Soviet long-range Bison bombers coming
from the Fili production plants were misleadingly numbered to make
the force appear much larger than it was.[12] He knew also that by
1960, the US atomic stockpile would have expanded to 1,000 weapons, and that the new Polaris submarines would be ready. Eisenhower accelerated plans for the deployment of Thor and Jupiter
medium-range missiles in Europe, and pushed the production sched-
ules of the American Atlas and Titan ICBMs.[13] But he refused to
distort the US economy by further massive spending on defence, even
though the Gaither Report had seductively suggested their recommendations would 'help sustain production and employment'.

Confident that national security was intact, Eisenhower's priorities
were strategic in a rather different sense. First, he wanted to mend the
breach with his bruised allies, Britain and France, and to sketch out
the ground rules for the changing relationship with the increasingly
confident Germany. And second, he understood that the shock of
Sputnik had created a vast expectation among the American people
for some form of reassuring response, and it had also pointed to a
useful long-term remedy. The Soviet investments in education and

science were impressive; the American education system could do with some improvement.

Perhaps the most enduring result of the Sputnik was America's National Defense Education Act of 1958, which began pumping $2 billion a year into what was frankly explained as a way to prevent the Russians from winning the brain race. After 1958, 25 per cent of construction costs on American campuses was financed by federal funds, and by 1960, the federal budget provided 20 per cent of university operating expenses (at Harvard, the figure was 25 per cent) and the taxpayer also paid for 70 per cent of university research.[14] By 1960, some 100,000 students were going to college with money borrowed from the government. This astonishing expansion of American university education was a direct result of a strategic decision by the national government. By 1960, there were 3.5 million students at America's institutions of higher learning. By 1970, there were 7 million, the result of 'a frenzied concern for national security'.[15]

The psychological shock of Sputnik hit Eisenhower all the harder because of the rift with his main European allies. The mood of estrangement after Suez was so intense that Dulles told the British Ambassador to Washington, Sir Harold Caccia, to call on him at home rather than invite comment by coming to the office.[16] But Eden had resigned, and the new British prime minister Harold Macmillan was an old wartime friend. He and Eisenhower had served together in North Africa after the Torch landings. After his appointment, as Macmillan went to the Turf Club to celebrate with oysters and champagne, he received a warm personal note from the White House: 'Remember the old adage, "Now abideth faith, hope and charity – and greater than these is a sense of humour." With warm regard, As ever, DE.'[17]

Inside the Foreign Office, a fundamental reassessment of Britain's position was under way, and its conclusions were formally submitted to the cabinet in January 1957. It acknowledged that the long pretence that Britain was still a great power was now demonstrably hollow. Even though Britain's own H-bomb was scheduled for its first test within three months, the weakness of the economy meant that the price of staying in the arms race would be bankruptcy. 'We should pool our resources with our European allies so that Western Europe as a whole might become a third nuclear power comparable with the US and the Soviet Union.'[18]

The British cabinet itself would not go quite so far. But as Macmillan embarked upon his premiership, he did so with a cabinet consensus that the old Atlantic relationship could no longer be trusted through thick and thin. It was time to consider the historic shift towards Europe, the cabinet minute recorded:[19]

> The Suez crisis had made it plain that there must be some change in the basis of Anglo-American relations. It was doubtful whether the US would now be willing to accord to us alone the special position which we had held as their principal ally during the war. We might therefore be better able to influence them if we were part of an association of Powers which had greater political, economic and military strength than we alone could command.

This was a half-hearted way to describe a strategic decision of such fundamental importance. More than a characteristic British compromise, the syntax of the cabinet decision reflected the deep reluctance with which it was made. Perhaps inevitably, compromise was what resulted. Macmillan, whose mother was American, counted a great deal on his personal ties with Eisenhower to restore the special relationship with America, while simultaneously exploring the new possibilities with Europe. In the same busy month of March 1957, Macmillan met Eisenhower at Bermuda and agreed to base sixty Thor missiles on British soil, and also met French premier Guy Mollet in Paris to discuss the Common Market.

At the same time, the young cabinet minister Reginald Maudling was instructed to carry out 'Plan G', the exploration of a European Free Trade Area, either as an alternative to, or including, the six members of the EEC. 'Be something of a St Paul, not merely the Jews but the Gentiles should be his care,' Macmillan wrote.[20] It was not so much that the British wanted to have it all ways – the American alliance, European free trade and Common Market too – but that in the wake of Suez, nothing seemed fixed, and all seemed fluid in a dangerously swirling world. As Macmillan recalled his first day in office, 'I had found our friendship with the United States destroyed, the European alliance almost shattered, and dismay and uncertainty in many parts of the Commonwealth.'[21]

By instinct, tradition and ancestry, and because Eisenhower's friendship was a lever which could redeem the problems in Europe and elsewhere, Macmillan resolved to mend his American fences first. And at Bermuda, the two elderly gentlemen relished their reunion, wandering in and out of each other's rooms in their pyjamas, chatting of old times and new challenges. Eisenhower was more than happy to make up, and later said the meeting had been 'by far the most successful international conference I had attended since the close of World War II'.[22]

Not only did they agree to base America's Thor missiles in Britain – for another four years the only US nuclear missiles that could reach the Soviet Union – but to equip them with a system of joint Anglo-American control. They were to be manned by British troops, but a dual key would be required to fire the weapons, one held by the Americans, the other by the British. Within the year, the Sputnik shock allowed Eisenhower to persuade Congress to erode the McMahon Act and share information with Britain on the design and manufacture of nuclear weapons, and also to share fissionable materials.[23] But nuclear weapons were not the only benefit of the special relationship which Macmillan had re-established; he needed American influence on a wider basis.

'The French have it in their power to wreck the European Free Trade Movement, and that in the long run must mean a further division of Europe, the probable end of Nato and most serious reorientation of British policy,' Macmillan wrote to Caccia, his Ambassador in Washington, asking him to arrange for the Americans to put pressure on the French. There was no certainty that the Common Market would actually develop. Philip de Zulueta, the Foreign Office liaison as Macmillan's private secretary, expressed the orthodox view: 'We really don't think the French and Germans will ever bury the hatchet to the extent of getting together to make the Common Market work.'[24]

Wrong-headed in retrospect, de Zulueta seemed right at the time. The French humiliation after Suez complicated the vicious war being fought in Algeria, which France insisted was no colony but a part of *la Patrie*. One of the French motives in attacking Egypt had been to stop Nasser's support for the Algerian independence movement, the FLN. After Suez, Nasser's support for the FLN intensified, and Soviet propaganda in the Middle East began, not unreasonably, to focus on Algeria as a symbol of Western imperialism. The war became increasingly controversial in France after *Le Monde* published the secret Béteille report, which acknowledged that the systematic use of torture was a central feature of the French campaign.[25]

In the two years after Suez, France gave every appearance of being ungovernable. Immediately after Macmillan's lunch with Guy Mollet, the French government fell, and there was no replacement for twenty-two days. Strikes and demonstrations against the Algerian war continued. *Le Monde*'s offices and the homes of its editors were fire-bombed. The dock-workers of Marseilles refused to unload the coffins of the conscripts. In May 1958, the French Army mounted a coup in Algeria, bringing on a political crisis in Paris, which was resolved only when General Charles de Gaulle was brought back to power. De Gaulle restored stability by killing off the Fourth Republic, and replacing it with a far more stable constitution which gave him as President sweeping powers to appoint and dismiss governments. In effect, he saved a kind of democracy in France by becoming a kind of dictator.

One of de Gaulle's first acts was to invite the US Commander of Nato forces, General Lauris Norstad, to give him and his military staff a full briefing on Nato deployments in France. Norstad did so, but spoke only of conventional weapons. De Gaulle then asked the American general to continue, spelling out the deployments of all the nuclear weapons in France, and their targets. De Gaulle's biographer recounts the momentous scene which ensued.

'Sir, I can answer only if we are alone,' Norstad said. 'So be it,' said de Gaulle. The two staffs withdrew. 'So then?' de Gaulle pressed. 'Then, Sir, I cannot reply to your questions, to my very great regret . . . ' And de Gaulle in conclusion: 'General, that is the last time, and make yourself understand it, that a responsible French leader will allow such a response to be made.'[26]

Technically under the terms of the Nato treaty, and under US law, General Norstad was right. But de Gaulle's country was in the front line of any Soviet attack. War would mean that those US nuclear bases on French soil would inevitably be targets for Soviet nuclear weapons. Nato prided itself on being an alliance of free states, in defence of the Free World, and not a Western version of the Warsaw Pact in which the Soviet Union dominated its satellites. The spirit of the Nato alliance entirely justified de Gaulle's cold fury. It was therefore an otiose and unnecessarily offensive non-reply which General Norstad gave to an allied head of state, when President Eisenhower was only a transatlantic phone call away.[27] Eisenhower had gone to great lengths to restore to the British that intimacy over nuclear affairs to which every British government had felt morally entitled since British physicists first persuaded President Roosevelt to launch the Manhattan Project, and helped to build the original atom bomb. Eisenhower could, and almost certainly would, have authorised Norstad to tell his old wartime comrade-in-arms whatever he needed to know. But that bizarre exchange between the American general, and the leader of an allied state he was sworn to help defend, foreshadowed the difficult decade which was to culminate in France's withdrawal from the military obligations of the Nato alliance, and the polite but firm request for all US troops to leave French soil, in 1966.

Behind de Gaulle's reaction lay a much deeper cause for concern, which was shared by the British. The technology of the ICBM transformed the strategic situation. It opened one possibility of a US–Soviet nuclear war, with the missiles passing over untouched European heads. It opened another, of the Soviets threatening a nuclear war with the United States in order to make gains in Europe. For de Gaulle, and indeed for all European leaders in private, there was a new nightmare, that the Kremlin might offer an American President the dreadful choice of surrendering Paris and Bonn without a fight, or risk losing Chicago. The ICBM imposed a monstrous burden of trust upon the Nato alliance and its nuclear deterrent. For the alliance to work, the Americans had to be able to convince the Europeans that they would be prepared to take nuclear hits on American cities, rather than abandon Western Europe.

In the aftermath of Suez, Western European leaders had good cause to ask themselves whether America would stick by them through thick and thin – particularly in the days before an American Presidential election. The question was acute for Adenauer's government in West Germany. For him, the immediate result of the Suez crisis was a visit to Bonn by Harold Macmillan to explain that the British air force in Germany was to be halved, and the army garrison reduced from 77,000 to 64,000 men.[28]

At the same time, George F. Kennan, America's intellectual father of the Cold War, was spending an academic year at Oxford, where he was invited to give the Reith Lectures for the BBC. Kennan suggested that it was time for both the United States and the Soviet Union to withdraw their troops from Germany, and leave it as a unified, demilitarised and neutral country. 'Until we stop pushing the Kremlin against a closed door, we shall never learn whether it will be prepared to go through an open one,' he suggested.[29] Back in the United States, James Burnham, that other Cold War intellectual who had opposed Kennan's containment policy as defeatist and had called for a policy of liberating Eastern Europe, startled conservative friends by agreeing with Kennan. Burnham too called for German neutrality, and a withdrawal of the troops.[30]

Such men were influential, which explains the stunning shock which greeted Adenauer in July 1958, when he received a personal letter from the American Secretary of State which began: 'My dear friend . . . ' Dulles went on to ask the West German Chancellor what he thought of a new idea to reduce the armaments of both sides in Germany 'through establishing significant zones of inspection which could greatly minimise the fear of massive surprise attack'. Dulles stopped some way short of suggesting unification, but this was the thin end of a wedge which led to demilitarisation of a freshly sovereign German state which had just won the right to rearm.[31]

Adenauer was appalled. Dulles, the man who had vowed 'to liberate the captive nations', was now conniving at their abandonment. The American commitment to Europe was suddenly, in these post-Suez and post-Sputnik days, far, far weaker than he had thought. The British were cutting back their forces. Adenauer's understandable reaction was to look to the only other support to hand, to France and de Gaulle, which meant to accept the French concept of Western Europe, and pay whatever economic price was required to the new Common Market in order to secure a French alliance.

Irony piled upon irony. The Western alliance had fallen into crisis because of the Anglo-French colonial adventure at Suez. Now both Britain and France were making amends. De Gaulle began taking the decisive step of abandoning French Algeria, and would face down another attempted military coup and a prolonged terrorist campaign in order to grant full independence in 1962. Under Harold Macmillan, Britain began quickly to divest itself of what had been the world's most extensive colonial empire. Ghana and Malaya were granted independence within the Commonwealth in 1957, Nigeria followed in 1960, and Kenya in 1963. More symbolically for Britain, and for that Western vulnerability to Soviet anti-colonial propaganda which so chafed American opinion, Macmillan made the divestiture with some generosity, considerable grace, and a ringing statement of decent principle. On his visit to South Africa, Macmillan addressed the parliament which had passed the racist legislation of apartheid, and announced:[32]

> The wind of change is blowing through this continent . . . As a fellow member of the Commonwealth it is our earnest desire to give South Africa our support and encouragement. But there are some aspects of your policies which make it impossible for us to do this without being false to our own deep conviction about the political destinies of free men, to which in our own territories we are trying to give effect.

And yet, having recognised with Suez that the game was up for colonial powers, Macmillan was simultaneously embarking on an unprecedented burst of gunboat diplomacy and troop deployments. The difference was that he was doing it in conjunction with the Americans, and doing so in the Middle East, to shore up some of those Western strategic and petroleum interests which had been imperilled after Suez. On 14 July 1958, General Abdel Karim Kassim led a military coup against the pro-British government of Iraq, and announced friendly relations with Nasser's latest diplomatic coup, the United Arab Republic. This was a loose federation of Egypt, Syria and Yemen, held together by little more than Nasser's Arab nationalist convictions. But the implications were momentous throughout the Middle East, not least in Lebanon, where pro-Nasser Muslims had begun a civil war against the Christians.

Eisenhower and Macmillan moved fast. British paratroops landed in Jordan, to shore up the nervous regime, and 14,000 US Marines waded ashore on the Lebanese beaches. They landed far enough from the fighting to be cheered by sunbathing women in bikinis. Dulles explained to the US Congress that 'recent Soviet political activities . . . [meant] . . . it was time to bring a halt to the deterioration in our position in the Middle East'.[33] Nasser flew to Moscow seeking support, and was refused. The new Iraqi government hastily announced that all oil contracts with Western companies remained in force.

Two years later, Iraq moved again, threatening to take over its '19th Province', the newly independent sheikhdom of Kuwait, just released from the British colonial yoke. The sheikh asked for the yoke to return in protective mode, and British troops flew back again. And at the southern end of the Persian Gulf, where the UAR member state of Yemen was supporting a nationalist movement in British-occupied Aden and in the colony of Muscat and Oman, British troops were reinforced yet again. The war in Oman was to sputter on well into the 1970s. And at the far end of the Indian Ocean, the British were about to deploy the largest military force they had sent overseas since 1945 to help defend the former colony of Malaysia against an aggressive Indonesia.[34]

Just as France was to deploy troops repeatedly in Africa in the 1960s and 1970s, so Britain was to find itself deploying troops to the Middle and Far East (and to Central America in the 1970s, during the Belize crisis with Guatemala) rather more frequently and into rather more danger after granting independence, than when trying to enforce its colonial grip. Just as Britain and France found themselves being forced to turn inwards to a strategic future in Europe, they were dispatching troops all across the old empires. But this was not bringing Britain and France any closer together. Macmillan's success at restoring his nuclear and strategic relationship with Eisenhower intensified de Gaulle's suspicion of the Anglo-Saxons. The closer Britain cleaved to America, the more de Gaulle leaned to Adenauer.

And Adenauer's alarm at the American fashion for theories of German neutralisation inclined him towards France.

'De Gaulle is bidding high for the hegemony of Europe,' Macmillan recorded in his diary, as de Gaulle invited Adenauer for a personal visit to his home at Colombey.[35] Perhaps. But de Gaulle was clearly seeking to build a Europe that could be independent of the arrogant Americans and their British Trojan Horse. The British were not prepared to make the European commitment, he told Adenauer. They should be excluded from the Common Market, and the Common Market should also stay out of that British plot for a European Free Trade Area. Under Macmillan's grandiose vision, this would include the Common Market and all the other nations, Austria, Denmark, Portugal, Switzerland, Norway and Sweden.

For de Gaulle, this was all a British ploy to weaken the Common Market into nothing more than a customs zone, and make Western Europe all the more vulnerable to the penetration of American capital. At Colombey, and during a return visit to Adenauer at Bad Kreuznach, de Gaulle engineered German support for the veto on British entry he finally announced on 14 November 1958. It was just six weeks before the Treaty of Rome came into force, to establish the European Economic Community and to seal Britain's exclusion. More tellingly, for the British and American assumption that the Soviet threat would eventually force de Gaulle back into line, his veto was announced four days after Khrushchev launched a new Berlin crisis, with the demand that Britain, France and the United States remove their 30,000 troops from West Berlin and make it into a free city.[36]

Something new was under way. In the Cold War's first decade, Western Europe had huddled together under American protection, and suspended most of the traditional jealousies for the greater imperative of survival. But the combination of strategic stability with prosperity in Europe brought back all of the old continent's pretensions, and its nationalist rivalries. The Suez adventure had been one symbol of this revival of European confidence. Another was that formal date of European economic recovery in 1958, the open convertibility of all their currencies against the dollar. The intra-European squabbles which followed Suez were yet another sign of maturity, albeit of an unhappy kind. It was a period of jostling for position between Britain, France and Germany, a revival of the culturally familiar nineteenth-century game of the European powers.

Suez and Sputnik, Dulles and de Gaulle, had combined to put the Western alliance under intense pressure in the late 1950s. But Nato and the West looked wholly cohesive by contrast with the disrepair in the Communist bloc. Indeed, the word bloc could hardly be applied to the region from Berlin to Beijing, after the twin blows of Khrushchev's de-Stalinisation and the Hungarian uprising. Khrushchev himself was almost toppled, the old guard in the Kremlin taking advantage of his visit to Finland in June 1957 to mount a palace coup within the Praesidium. It failed, in part because Marshal Zhukov was on Khrushchev's side, and made military aircraft available to fly back to Moscow the far-flung members of the Communist Party Central Committee. But the real significance of Khrushchev's victory was that it depended upon a form of party democracy. Khrushchev simply refused to accept that the Praesidium had the right to sack him. He had been elected General Secretary by the Central Committee; only they could dismiss him. He insisted that a full plenum of the committee be assembled, and vowed to abide by the result. Khrushchev won overwhelmingly.

This was one striking illustration of how matters had changed since the de-Stalinisation speech. The second was the fate of Khrushchev's enemies. They were not shot or dispatched to the Gulag. Molotov was demoted to Ambassador to Mongolia, Malenkov was appointed manager of an electric-power plant, and Kaganovich was made director of a cement factory. Kaganovich even telephoned Khrushchev, tearfully begging him 'not to allow them to deal with me as they dealt with people under Stalin'. Khrushchev replied: 'You will be given a job. You will be able to work and live in peace if you work honestly like all Soviet people.'[37] That at least was the version Khrushchev gave to the twenty-second Party Congress. And certainly, all the conspirators of what was called the Anti-Party Group lived, even if not permitted to tell their tale.

China had been appalled by the attacks upon Stalin, disappointed by the modesty of Soviet economic help, and increasingly worried at Khrushchev's attempts at *détente* ever since the Geneva summit of 1955. There were two distinct themes to Chinese policy after 1956. The first was self-reliance. 'China must rely upon her own resources as much as possible,' declared Li Fu-chun, chairman of the State Planning Commission, in May 1957. His colleague, Po Yi-po, chairman of the State Economic Commission, took the sentiment further, announcing that China must 'reduce reliance on foreign countries'.[38]

The second theme was that the newly evident Soviet technological superiority meant, in Mao's words to the Moscow conference on the anniversary of the October Revolution: 'The international situation has now reached a turning point. There are two winds in the world today, the East wind and the West wind . . . I think the characteristic of the situation today is the East wind prevailing over the West wind.'[39] And from there, it was but a short step to the new image of the West that became a cliché of the Chinese press, that the imperialists were paper tigers.[40]

Mao's blithe readiness to accept the inevitability of a nuclear war, and its possible utility as a way to bring about the final defeat of capitalism, stunned his comrades from other countries. According to China's later denunciations of Moscow, it was during this conference that the Soviet leadership agreed in principle to give China uranium-enrichment facilities and a demonstration model of the atom bomb. It was never delivered: Mao's immediate reaction may have given them pause for thought.[41] Shmuel Mikunis, the leader of the Israeli Communist Party, recorded a conversation in the Kremlin between Mao and Palmiro Togliatti, the Italian party leader:[42]

> Togliatti then asked him: 'But what would become of Italy as a result of such a war?' Mao Tse-tung looked at him in a thoughtful way and replied, quite coolly, 'But who told you that Italy must survive? Three hundred million Chinese will be left, and that will be enough for the human race to continue.'

Throughout 1957, as the Chinese party operated under Mao's permissive slogan 'Let a hundred flowers bloom', it was assumed in Moscow as in the West that China was undergoing its own version of de-Stalinisation and relaxation. But within months, in the words of one young Central Committee official in Moscow, 'having allowed the hundred flowers to bloom, the Chinese leadership began mercilessly to mow them down, and the new policy began to look like a provocation'.[43] Just as Khrushchev was hoping to assert the unity of the Communist world, and contrast it with the disarray of the West, China then put intense pressure on Khrushchev to condemn Yugoslavia for 'revisionism'. Khrushchev acceded, as the price of maintaining his ties with China. But then these too began to fray, as China plunged into a double crisis, at home and on its nervous coastline.

The Chinese economy had never recovered from the civil war, and the attempts to impose collective farms on a vast country with poor communications proved disastrously inefficient. The Chinese leadership, after an angry internal debate, decided on the massive gamble of the Great Leap Forward. The goal was to concentrate twenty years of Soviet-style development into a single year. The method was draconian, to militarise the land, reducing 700,000 collective farms into 26,000 communes. Each unit of 20,000 peasants became the farming equivalent of an army division, and disciplined in military fashion. In the cities, the disappointing industrial production was to be doubled by exploiting backyard industry, asking blacksmiths to do the work of miniature steel mills.

While this giant and ultimately abortive upheaval was under way, China began shelling the offshore islands of Quemoy and Matsu, occupied by the forces of Taiwan. The American Seventh Fleet shipped Taiwanese reinforcements to the islands, and provided extra artillery capable, at least in theory, of firing atomic shells. Mao appealed for Soviet nuclear weapons; Khrushchev responded only with assurances, that the Soviet Union would come to China's support if the Americans actually attacked.[44]

For China, this was betrayal. For Khrushchev: 'We didn't want to give them the idea we were their obedient slaves, who would give them whatever they wanted, no matter how much they insulted us.'[45] Fundamental differences between Beijing and Moscow also developed over the levels of Soviet aid, and above all over the way to respond to the US–British show of force in the Middle East in 1958. China, which seemed to have an overblown view of the strategic superiority the Sputnik implied, was adamant. China's official *People's Daily* declared: 'There cannot be the slightest indulgence towards American imperialism's act of aggression.' Khrushchev, who knew that the Soviet armed forces at that time had in fact a very modest nuclear arsenal of about one hundred warheads, and fewer than thirty missiles to deliver them, appealed for a summit with Eisenhower.[46]

'Our country and the United States are the two most mighty powers in the world. If other countries fight among themselves, they can be separated. But if war breaks out between American and our country, no one will be able to stop it. It will be a catastrophe on a colossal scale,' Khrushchev told a party rally in Dnepropetrovsk, shortly before his trip to the United States finally took place in 1959.[47] He had made a similar point to a visiting group of American state governors shortly before that. He seems to have been entirely genuine in his realisation of how dreadful a nuclear war would be, and firmly opposed to granting such weapons to the less restrained Chairman Mao. So how are we to explain Khrushchev's occasional forays into the kind of brinkmanship which appeared to risk nuclear war? His threat to Britain and France at the time of Suez may have been empty. But it could have provoked that American nuclear response which we know Eisenhower was steeling himself to make, if missiles actually landed on London and Paris. Khrushchev's spasmodic provocations over Berlin may seem a lesser kind of crisis. But he kept jabbing at that nerve, with his demand for a withdrawal of Western troops in 1958, the building of the Berlin Wall, and the sudden stand-off between US and Soviet tanks in 1961. Any such confrontation always carried the risk of unexpected escalation, of junior commanders panicking and shooting, of a process getting under way which might easily escape the control of the cooler heads in Washington and Moscow.

Khrushchev's Berlin campaign was seen by one of the key Americans who had to face it, President Kennedy's national security adviser McGeorge Bundy, as a logical result of the Sputnik event. For the White House, the Berlin crisis was: 'A Soviet exercise in atomic diplomacy . . . an effort to use a new appearance of Soviet nuclear strength to force changes in the center of Europe.'[48] It was the first deliberate nuclear challenge by the Kremlin, a foray into the world of risk and what Dulles had labelled brinkmanship. A complexity of motives were at work here: the pride of the Soviet military; the Kremlin's determination to be seen to command American respect; the temptation to test the depth of American resolve, and the cohesion of the Nato alliance, by some nuclear pressure. A final factor may have been Khrushchev's own internal jostling with political rivals and constituencies, in the Soviet Union and perhaps in China.

But the Americans too played at brinkmanship. The United States under Truman had rattled the nuclear sabre when it first sent B-29 bombers to Britain at the time of the Berlin blockade. President Eisenhower made another nuclear flourish to bring about an armistice in Korea. He and Dulles had done so again, perhaps more discreetly, when Britain refused to join them in support of the French in Vietnam at the time of Dien Bien Phu, to force the Vietminh and the Chinese to the Geneva negotiating table. Rather less discreet was the dispatch of nuclear-capable artillery to Quemoy and Matsu in 1958. To the Kremlin, these were clear messages, whether explicit threats through diplomatic channels, or mobilisations and deployments of nuclear-capable forces. Both sides were gaining experience in this delicate game of 'exercises in nuclear diplomacy'.

The same complexity of motives that can be ascribed to Khrushchev came into play in the White House. Eisenhower had allies to reassure, and military and political constituencies in Congress and the Pentagon, to appease. He too came under occasionally intense military pressure, particularly at the time of Dien Bien Phu, to use nuclear weapons. The US Air Force chief of staff, General Nathan Twining, was all for it: 'I don't think that three small A-bombs placed properly would have caused too much trouble or set a precedent, but it would have taught those Chinese a good lesson, we would have saved the French and perhaps our present difficulties in Southeast Asia could have been avoided,' the general recalled for the Dulles oral history project. 'I still think it would have been a good idea.'[49]

In spite of all these motives that impelled them into the risky arena of nuclear diplomacy, there is no sign that Eisenhower or Khrushchev was ever seriously prepared to initiate the final step towards war. But each man was also, for reasons of personal and national prestige, reluctant to be seen to back down at any point. The stakes involved in nuclear diplomacy were so great that each leader during a crisis was poised on an uneasy see-saw, having to keep a tenuous balance between sinking into war on the one side, or into a perceived kind of surrender on the other. A subtle gamesmanship came into play as each side began to invent entirely new rules of etiquette in this nuclear world. While it was tempting to see the other side lose balance and fall into a retreat which signalled humiliation, it was also dangerous. Too hasty an attempt to restore equilibrium after tilting towards surrender could send the see-saw plunging fast the other way. It became almost as important to save the other side's face in a crisis as to save one's own. The basic rule of this new game was that it had to be kept going; to end it could mean the end of the world.

The difficulty in maintaining this nuclear balance was that so many unpredictable weights would suddenly land on one end or the other of each side's see-saw. The allies, for wholly internal reasons that had nothing to do with the US–Soviet balance, could suddenly send their leaders teetering on the brink of losing control. The Anglo-French invasion of Suez was but the first and most dramatic of these sudden shocks to stability. China was just as unpredictable for Moscow. Just as Khrushchev began angling for a summit meeting with Eisenhower in 1958, the Quemoy–Matsu crisis blew up off the Chinese coastline, and the Iraqi officer corps decided to mount their military coup.

The nuclear balance was constantly at risk from the unexpected. On the first day of the new year of 1959, Fidel Castro's guerrillas seized power in Cuba after four years of fighting. At least the Cuban crisis took some months to build, time for both Khrushchev and the United States to start making some assessments of the dangers and opportunities that a pro-Soviet Cuba might present. Oddly enough, these slow-building but constant crises proved far more dangerous than the sudden storms in the Middle or Far East that came without warning. The two most dangerous moments in the nuclear relationship came over Berlin and over Cuba, two flashpoints in which the superpowers had the luxury of time to establish their priorities and their policies.

In the case of Berlin, they even had the benefit of a rehearsal. The Soviet government had every reason to try to settle the still unresolved question of a peace treaty that would formally end World War Two and establish the frontiers of Eastern Europe. Khrushchev's proposal contained a good deal of sense. He suggested that the USA, UK, France and Soviet Union all sign with the two Germanies a peace treaty which recognised the de facto frontiers. This would open the way for the Polish and Czech frontiers to be ratified too. Recognising that Berlin was a problem, with the island of West Berlin still surrounded by what Khrushchev called the German Democratic Republic, he proposed making Berlin a free city. It would be demilitarised and self-governing, its integrity and access to the outside world guaranteed by the four powers and both Germanies.

For the West, this entailed an insurmountable legal problem. It would mean that the land access to Berlin would pass from the control of the Soviet Union, a fellow signatory of the four-power occupation agreement of 1945, to the sovereign government of a newly recognised East Germany. The implications of such a move also worried the West. It would signal a retreat from an outpost that had been so staunchly defended during the Berlin airlift. It would set a precedent of Western withdrawal from West German interests, and from the principle of eventual German unification. It would also remove from the heart of the Soviet Empire a Western outpost, glittering in prosperity and beaming out radio waves and TV transmissions of the capitalist promise. It would close an extremely useful intelligence listening post, and it would dismay the West German allies, who were at the heart of both Nato and the new EEC.

These were not considerations the West chose to over-publicise, so they stuck by the legal argument, even when Khrushchev in his impatience set a six-month deadline for the West to agree. The alternative, he declared, was that he would sign his own independent peace treaty with East Germany, and let the West worry about negotiating their own access past East German border guards. All this was put with characteristic bluntness, and in his meeting with Chancellor Adenauer, the Soviet Ambassador was deliberately offensive, as Soviet officials usually were when dealing with West Germans. Adenauer could never forget his first meeting with Khrushchev, in Moscow in 1955. Adenauer was seeking the return of the estimated 130,000 German POWs still in the Soviet Union. In response to Adenauer's request Khrushchev snapped that there were only 10,000, all of them Nazi war criminals. When Adenauer persisted, Khrushchev shouted at him to remember the Italians who had come on the German side to invade Russia. They had gone home too – all in coffins.[50]

So on 11 March, President Eisenhower found himself at a White House press conference being asked if the United States was prepared to conduct a nuclear war if necessary to defend free Berlin. Eisenhower picked his words with care: 'I didn't say that nuclear war is a complete impossibility. I said it couldn't, as I see it, free anything . . . We have got to stand right ready and say, We will do what is necessary to protect ourselves, but we are never going to back up on our rights and responsibilities.'[51]

It was a neat encapsulation of the nuclear dilemma. The weapons were, in themselves, so destructive that they were militarily useless. They could not free anything, only eradicate it. But the issues on which they stood guard went to the very core of a state's identity and interest. They could neither be rationally used, nor rationally forsworn. The trick was to identify one's own core interests, and those of the nuclear adversary, and be careful not to trespass upon them. Years later, in retirement, Eisenhower told his biographer, 'There is nothing in the world that the Communists want badly enough to risk losing the Kremlin.'[52] This was true, but missed half the point. The trick of nuclear diplomacy was to define what, whether territory or allies or that elusive oriental concept of face, the Soviet leadership would so dread losing that they might indeed prefer to risk losing the Kremlin.

That first Berlin crisis was settled when Khrushchev dropped his deadline once Eisenhower agreed to negotiate, and to invite Khrushchev to the United States. The very fact that he had done so suggested that Soviet nuclear diplomacy was working, that West Berlin was a nerve that the Soviets could irritate as and when they chose. But the problem of losing face now began to afflict the American side. Sputnik was in the sky, and was now joined by a new satellite weighing 1.5 tonnes, which made the military potential of a Soviet ICBM brutally clear. America was still discussing the Gaither Report, and doing so on the basis of that best-seller of 1959, *The Uncertain Trumpet*, the explosive book by the former US Army chief of staff, General Maxwell Taylor.

General Taylor argued that the doctrine of 'massive retaliation' had run its course, and 'could offer our leaders only two choices, the initiation of general nuclear war, or compromise and retreat'. The book was a passionate argument for a more flexible and much larger military force, capable of fighting effectively various levels of war, regional or global, without having to resort to nuclear weapons. And it concluded with a warning from one familiar with the Gaither Report: 'It must be made clear to our citizens that the nation will face a serious crisis beginning about 1961. For a period of years thereafter, the balance of military strength will tip dangerously in favour of the Communist bloc unless we take drastic action now.'[53]

Taylor's call, with all the authority of one of the country's leading generals, became one of the texts of the 1960 Presidential election campaign. Each of the three Democratic candidates, Senator Lyndon Johnson of Texas, Senator Stuart Symington of Missouri, and Senator John F. Kennedy of Massachusetts, campaigned hard on the missile gap. Kennedy, who won the Democratic nomination, was by far the most hawkish on the size of the gap, on its strategic implications, and on the evil nature of the enemy. 'The enemy is the Communist system itself – implacable, insatiable, unceasing in its drive for world domination,' ran the speech with which he opened the autumn campaign, at the Mormon Tabernacle in Salt Lake City. 'This is not a struggle for supremacy of arms alone. It is also a struggle for supremacy between two conflicting ideologies; freedom under God versus ruthless, godless tyranny.'[54]

In his stump speech of the campaign, the core message which he repeated at every stop along the campaign trail, Kennedy promised a programme of rearmament that would ensure that the United States would not lose that struggle. 'We will mould our strength and become first again. Not first if. Not first but. Not first when. But first period. I want the world to wonder not what Mr Khrushchev is doing. I want them to wonder what the United States is doing.'[55]

There was no missile gap, and Kennedy knew it. Eisenhower had arranged for the Democratic candidate to be briefed by CIA Director Allen Dulles, by Strategic Air Command, and by the joint chiefs at the Pentagon. They all told Kennedy the same thing. Khrushchev might claim that his factories were turning out missiles like so many sausages. He was not. The main Soviet nuclear strength lay in medium-range missiles that threatened the whole of Nato Europe, and in long-range manned bombers that were a threat, but not a crippling one. Of ICBMs that could reach the United States, there were but a handful, and they were being produced very slowly. In fact, US intelligence later established that only four examples of the first model of Soviet ICBM had been built.[56] By contrast, the first Polaris missile-armed submarine, the *George Washington*, became operational in 1960. Within two years, there were eight more at sea, carrying a total of 144 nuclear-tipped missiles which were invulnerable to Soviet retaliation.

Much of Khrushchev's nuclear diplomacy was based on bluff, and the credibility given to that bluff by Sputnik. For the world public, Soviet pre-eminence in missiles was further established in September 1959 when Khrushchev marked his arrival in the United States with the impact of the Lunik, a Soviet research missile, upon the surface of the Moon. When they met, he thoughtfully presented President Eisenhower with a replica of the Soviet pennant the Lunik had carried.[57] Although little was decided in their meetings, Khrushchev returned to Moscow waxing lyrical about 'the spirit of Camp David', the President's country retreat, where they had at least agreed to meet again in a four-power summit the following year.

The Soviet missile bluff could not be long sustained after 1956, when the US Air Force bought forty-eight single-seater models of Lockheed's U-2 spy-plane, and five two-seater models. Flying too high for Soviet anti-aircraft missiles or fighters, they roamed the skies above the Soviet Union with impunity after 1957.[58] From bases in Japan, Turkey and Britain, they stayed in the air for twelve hours, mapping and photographing the vast land mass, its air and missile bases and factories. Eisenhower's scepticism of the missile gap was based on hard evidence. He had been charmed and convinced of the powers of the U-2 when the CIA gave him a photograph of himself playing golf at Augusta, taken from 70,000ft. He could even discern the golfball.[59] But the evidence was never quite complete, and in 1960, as Eisenhower prepared for a new summit with Khrushchev in Paris, the CIA pressed for one last mission, to establish whether there might be a missile plant or base near the Urals, in an area which had only been sketchily surveyed. It was a mission too many; the latest version of anti-aircraft missiles finally caught up with the American technology.

On 5 May, as the summit was about to begin, Khrushchev announced that a U-2 had been shot down over Soviet territory. The immediate American reaction was to deny that it had been on a spy mission, but had merely lost its way. This thin tale Khrushchev triumphantly refuted by producing the pilot, Gary Powers, his suicide needle, cameras, and irrefutable evidence that this had been an espionage mission. Eisenhower accepted responsibility, and declared in Paris that the spy flights had taken place with his full knowledge. Khrushchev was evidently determined to take maximum advantage of the event, even if the summit collapsed. He insisted on an American apology, a promise not to do it again, and that 'the criminals be

punished'. Eisenhower refused. De Gaulle pointed out that modern
technology was making sovereignty over a state's higher airspace a
more and more elusive concept; a Soviet satellite, he pointed out, was
orbiting over France. Macmillan tried to reach a compromise, but
then sank into gloom and the pages of his comforting Jane Austen
novel.[60] The Paris summit never took place.

The thaw was over, and the spirit of Camp David had expired. A
month later, the Soviet delegation walked out of the Geneva disarma-
ment talks, where Macmillan had been pushing hard for a nuclear-test
control agreement. Macmillan, de Gaulle and Eisenhower were all
baffled by the vigour of the Soviet reaction. But then the Commonwealth proved its worth. Tunku Abdul Rahman of Malaysia wrote to
Macmillan to suggest that the Soviet hard line was less to do with
East–West relations than with the growing crisis in Sino-Soviet
affairs.[61] Macmillan had never thought of that. Two weeks after the
Tunku's letter, Khrushchev delivered his first open attack upon the
Chinese with an eighty-page letter of denunciation at the Bucharest
conference of the Romanian party.[62] The Sino-Soviet split was public.

The split had been coming for at least two years, but Khrushchev
had tried to paper it over. He had kept silent when Chinese troops
crossed the Indian frontier, and scattered the Indian forces, in August.
Immediately after the Camp David meeting with Eisenhower, Khrushchev had flown to Beijing for a disastrous visit. The Chinese
denounced his casual statement that Eisenhower evidently enjoyed
the support of the American public. This was dangerous ground.
Khrushchev was not so secure in Moscow that he could afford a split
with China, at least on the grounds that he was being too conciliatory
to the West. There were enough among the Soviet generals and the
party who might agree, or find that argument a useful lever to pry him
from office. Khrushchev's retort that his policy of *détente* would yield
useful results was unproven. There was no sign of any settlement on
the German question, and the provocative American spy flights
continued. With the U-2 scalp hanging from the belts of his proud
generals, Khrushchev found it politically expedient to take their side.

He had tested his generals' loyalty far enough. In the four years
after the de-Stalinisation speech, the Soviet armed forces had been
reduced from 5.8 million to 3.6 million men. Shortly after Marshal
Zhukov had saved Khrushchev's political life during the attempted
palace coup of June 1957, Khrushchev had sacked Zhukov, who was
dangerously powerful, and replaced him with Marshal Malinovsky.
At the same time, he accelerated the military cuts, retired over 14,000
officers, and imposed a new degree of party control by establishing a

main Political Directorate for Army and Navy as a department of the party's Central Committee apparatus. In January 1960, at the Supreme Soviet session, he announced a further deep cut of 1.2 million men, reducing the Soviet armed forces to 2.4 million in total, their lowest level since 1938.[63] Khrushchev argued that missiles and nuclear weapons meant that the nature of Soviet security no longer relied on mass armies, but the social effects of this cut were highly disruptive. Almost 100,000 officers and even more veteran NCOs were dismissed, and many of them were left homeless and unemployed for a prolonged period. The morale of the conventional armed forces sank, even as the party's political control over them tightened, and the promotions and the remaining budgets were lavished on the new arm of the Strategic Rocket Forces. In this context, it is evident why Khrushchev held off the Sino-Soviet split as long as he could, and tried to maintain something of that spirit of Camp David with which he justified his defence cuts.

Equally, it is clear why Khrushchev gave up on the lame-duck President Eisenhower, when he knew he would face a vigorous new generation in the White House within six months. The choice was already becoming evident, between Vice-President Richard Nixon, who had led the persecution of Alger Hiss and the American left, or Senator Kennedy, who was campaigning on the need to close the missile gap. Neither one was promising. But if Khrushchev was beset by the schism with the Chinese, the Americans had new difficulties in their own back yard. Nixon had been mobbed by anti-American demonstrators in Venezuela, and the Americans had a new enemy. In July 1960, alarmed at the course of the new government of Fidel Castro in Cuba, they cut Cuba's sugar quota from the US market. The Soviet Union signed a trade pact to buy Cuban sugar in exchange for petrol and technical help. For Khrushchev, the American alarm was a Soviet opportunity: 'They feared, as much as we hoped, that a socialist Cuba might become a magnet that would attract other Latin American countries to socialism.'[64] Exactly: the pattern of the new confrontation with the new American President was set.

Chapter 6

The Torch Has Been Passed

You above all who have come to the far end, victims
Of a run-down machine, who can bear it no longer;
Whether in easy chairs chafing at impotence
Or against hunger, bullies and spies perserving
The nerve for action, the spark of indignation –
Need fight in the dark no more, you know your enemies.
You shall be leaders when zero hour is signalled,
Wielders of power and welders of a new world.

'The Magnetic Mountain', C. Day Lewis

The central importance of the Cold War to politicians, generals and state officials was not always apparent to the taxpayers who sustained them. By most standards of statesmanship, the British Conservative governments which had been in office throughout most of the decade of the 1950s had performed miserably. They had exposed the nation to an unprecedented international humiliation at Suez. The old colonial empire, source of so much pride that the wall maps in the state schools were still dominated by great swathes of imperial crimson, was being divested apace. Britain's former command of the oil resources of Iran and Iraq had been sharply curtailed.

The government had failed in its attempt to persuade the whole of Western Europe to join a free-trade area, and its belated scratching at the door of the European Economic Community had been rebuffed. The alternative of the Atlantic Alliance was still clutched, and American nuclear bases on British soil, where a token Royal Air Force officer was nominal camp commander but where British laws no longer ran, were now a permanent feature. But Suez had revealed the limits of American forbearance and support. In the great game of nations, the Conservative governments had played a series of losing hands. And yet they were triumphantly re-elected to office in October 1959, increasing their majority over all other parties in the House of Commons from 67 to 107 seats.

The explanation lay in economics, and the growth of prosperity, astutely exploited by the advertising firm of Coleman, Prentice & Varley. Hired for the unprecedented fee of £500,000 to sell the Conservative cause to the public, they pasted on billboards across the country the slogan: 'Life's Better Under the Conservatives – Don't Let Labour Ruin It'. Macmillan's own throwaway remark, 'You've never had it so good', may have enjoyed more popular resonance. The growth rate of the 1950s averaged slightly less than 3 per cent a year. This was good by British standards, and sufficient to win the 1959 election. But by comparison with the Western European economies, this growth rate was feeble, and it spelled relative decline. The British growth rate of the 1950s averaged something between one-third and one-half of the growth rates enjoyed by Italy (5.9 per cent annually) or Germany (7.6 per cent) during the same period. Prime Minister Harold Macmillan's reaction to this was both resigned and rather weary: 'Of course, if we succeeded in losing two world wars, wrote off all our debts – instead of having nearly £30,000 million in debts – got rid of all our foreign obligations, and kept no force overseas, then we might be as rich as the Germans.'[1]

When writing his first letter, of congratulation and amicable advice, to the newly elected President Kennedy, Macmillan made clear his conviction that economics lay at the very heart of the confrontation with Communism. It was not simply that wealth was essential to buy weapons and military research, but that the Cold War itself was a form of economic competition. He began by suggesting to Kennedy that the Atlantic Alliance was 'not properly adjusted to the realities of the 1960s', and went on to warn that this was a race the West could yet lose. Macmillan did not say so, but the Soviet economy in the 1950s had been growing more than twice as fast as the British.

The main question, Macmillan suggested to the President-elect, was:[2]*

> what is going to happen to us unless we can show that our modern free society – the new form of capitalism – can make the fullest use of our resources and results in a steady expansion of our economic strength . . . If we fail in this, Communism will triumph, not by war, or even subversion, but by seeming to be a better way of bringing

---

* This letter to Kennedy was deemed important enough for Professor J. K. Galbraith to be summoned to the Oval Office to discuss its implications. When Galbraith arrived, the letter could not be found. The White House was turned upside down, until the document was finally located in the nursery of Caroline, the President's three-year-old daughter.

people material comforts. In other words, if we were to fall back into anything like the recession or crisis that we had between the wars, with large-scale unemployment of men and machines, I think we would have lost the hand.

Macmillan's 'new form of capitalism' was the mixed economy, which depended on a blend of private enterprise and strategic intervention by the state. The state was able to direct national resources to provide a welfare safety net for its citizens, to support chosen industries, and to manipulate the money supply and interest rate to speed or slow the economy. It was based very largely on the theoretical work of Keynes, and on the practical lessons of the Great Depression of the 1930s. Governments took the big decisions, as Eisenhower had done to build the Interstate road network, or to pass the post-Sputnik Education Acts, or to spend their way out of recessions.

With an economy as dominant as that of the USA, the state could also deploy its investments into building up the economies of whole continents. Europe was thriving after the Marshall Plan, Japan was booming after the Korean War 'Special Procurements'. To have been an official in the US State Department or in the Treasury in the 1950s was to have felt, quite literally, like a master of the universe. The global economy lay there, waiting to be kissed into glowing life by an astute deployment of the US dollar. There were recessions and bumps along the road, to be sure. But the self-assurance of governments that their economies could be steered into self-sustaining growth was remarkable, a modern equivalent of that sublime Victorian faith in 'progress'. It seemed, as Macmillan had written to Kennedy, that governments had at last found the golden key to endless economic growth.

But other words were ringing simultaneously in the new President's ears. As John Kennedy came into office in that cold January of 1961, Eisenhower had delivered a farewell address that was uncharacteristically thoughtful, and sobering. He warned that the Cold War had produced something 'new in American experience . . . the conjunction of an immense military establishment and a large arms industry . . . [its] influence is felt in every city, every state house, every office in the federal government . . . In the councils of government, we must guard against the acquisition of unwarranted influence, whether sought or unsought, by the military–industrial complex.'[3]

The awesome weight of the defence budget in the American economy had weighed heavily on Eisenhower. In 1960, defence expenditure took 52.2 per cent of federal spending,[4] or just over 10 per cent of

GDP. It had been even higher, peaking at 12.7 per cent of GDP in 1954, and the Eisenhower Administration's reliance on the doctrine of 'massive retaliation' had been justified as a cheaper way of deterring the Communists. It was still expensive, and as Eisenhower warned, budgets of that size created powerful political and institutional constituencies. They were to be found in trade unions as in the Pentagon; among real-estate developers around the booming new defence plants of Texas and Georgia and California; and among the politicians whose electors worked in them. They all sought to ensure that the money continued to flow. Wall Street too enjoyed the Cold War. Aerospace stocks rose in value, three times higher than the stock-market average, between 1947 and 1956.[5]

Sums of this size – and the US defence budget was for the first two decades of the Cold War about half the size of the entire British economy – not only generate their own supporters. The ability to control and direct a defence budget worth 10 per cent of American GDP also gave governments a powerful lever to stimulate the rest of the economy. Keynes's theory of government intervention in the economy, and Eisenhower's military–industrial complex, combined in a marriage made in that heaven of Harold Macmillan's 'New Capitalism'. The Gaither Report had already made this explicit, talking of the beneficial impact upon the economy of the massive civil-defence project it recommended.

Even without such a programme, the Cold War was transforming the industrial geography of the United States, and shifting the new manufacturing base to the Sunbelt. The southern and western states had right-to-work laws, which weakened the role of trade unions. The South also enjoyed stable state politics, which meant that sheer longevity had won them the chairmanship of the key Congressional committees where the Pentagon's spending decisions were made. Lyndon Johnson of Texas was the Senate Majority leader, and Georgia's Richard Russell and Carl Vinson ran the Senate and House armed services committees between them. The resulting symbiosis brought the Houston space centre to Texas, where Bell helicopters and the Vought division of LTV Industries also boomed. Georgia's boom came with military bases, and the Lockheed plants at Marietta.

Since World War Two, the aerospace industry had been building new industrial bases away from the traditional industrial heartland of the north-east and the Great Lakes. The long military spending boom and the McDonnell–Douglas, North American and Hughes Aircraft plants helped explode the Californian population sixfold in the five decades after 1940, while Boeing expanded in the north-west. General

Dynamics and McDonnell–Douglas helped create another regional
military–industrial complex in St Louis. And in the name of national
security, and justified in terms of the need to evacuate the cities in a
nuclear alert, all of these new industrial centres were linked into a
continent-wide grid through the Interstate highway network.

A similar process, far more intensively planned and ruthlessly
directed, was under way in the Soviet Union. Like the growth of
California, it had begun during World War Two, but in more urgent
circumstances. In one of the most remarkable transmigrations in
industrial history, the Soviet system dismantled and evacuated a total
of 1,523 strategic factories from the path of the advancing Germans in
the winter of 1941–2, and shipped them to the new industrial areas
beyond the Urals, out of bombing range. Just over 700 of them were
rebuilt in a vast new industrial zone around Sverdlovsk and Chelya-
binsk, which was to become a nuclear weapons development complex
in the 1950s. Another 350 factories were shipped across the Caspian
Sea to Kazakhstan, where a new coal and steel zone was humming at
Karaganda. And another 200 of these arms and machine-tool plants
were transported over the Trans-Siberian railway to the Soviet Far
East.[6]

The cataracts of defence spending and investment in the three most
heavily armed states, the USA, Britain and the Soviet Union, produced
oddly contradictory economic effects. The investments in armaments
plants spurred the raw statistics of 'growth', but only in the way that
those deceptive statistics would record a car accident as 'growth'
because of the economic activity generated by the towing firms, the
hospitals and the insurance companies. There were some hugely
important exceptions, where military technology transferred directly
into the civilian economy. The benefits were evident in electronics,
satellites and the Boeing 707 jet airliner, which began life as a military
refuelling tanker for Strategic Air Command.

But much of the military spending was economically hollow. The
defence-industry payrolls may have enriched California and Texas
and Sverdlovsk, yet the output of those plants did not generate more
growth in the civilian economy. The products of the defence economy
found their justification mainly in the protection they provided the
civilian economy which financed it. The tanks and aircraft and
submarines went to training camps and airfields, were crashed or
destroyed, mothballed and finally broken up for scrap. They gave the
appearance of power, but over the years the diversion of research and
manpower investment resources into the defence industries eroded
that power's financial base. The fastest-growing economy of the

period, Japan, never spent more than 1 per cent of GDP on defence. West Germany's defence budget peaked at 5 per cent of GDP in 1965, but fell below 4 per cent in 1975 and remained there. The economy which invested the most in defence spending, the Soviet Union, proved over the long term to be the most damaged by this distorted allocation of resources.[7]

The burden of superpower status was already becoming apparent in the United States as John Kennedy took the oath of inauguration as President in January 1961. The steady leakage of gold from Fort Knox had become so worrisome that he told one visitor that the two things that troubled him most were nuclear war and the payments deficit. It was, if not money well spent, then money with a strategic purpose behind it; what one historian called 'the expenses of running a Pax Americana'.[8]

In 1946, at the end of World War Two, the US held 60 per cent of the world's gold reserves. By 1949, the US share had risen to 72 per cent, in part because of the onerous repayment terms imposed on the British for post-war loans. To this degree, the Marshall Plan's effusion of dollars into Europe was forced by the way US economic dominance drained Europe of gold and dollars in the immediate post-war years. The Marshall Plan, and the later foreign-exchange costs of keeping US troops overseas, reversed the situation. The United States ran a constant balance-of-payments deficit throughout this period, and financed those deficits not with gold, but in paper dollars. Those paper dollars were, however, backed by gold. If the Europeans suspected that the dollars might not be sound, they were legally entitled to demand gold from the vaults at Fort Knox.[9]

The cautious Europeans, and in particular France, suspected that this paper financing might eventually end in a dollar devaluation. As a result, between 1949 and 1959, they used the US dollars piling up in their banks and their treasuries to purchase $5.7 billion of gold from the US. The US financial authorities had brought this upon themselves, with the post-war economic system that was devised at the Bretton Woods conference. As the world's reserve currency, the US dollar had to finance the emerging global economy. Robert Solomon, of the Federal Reserve Board, noted in retrospect: 'Of the $8.5 billions increase in world reserves in the years 1949–59, the US provided $7 billions through the increase in its liabilities to foreign monetary authorities.'[10]

As Kennedy took office, the balance-of-payments deficit was $2 billion, and gold was leaving Fort Knox at a rate of $1.5 billion a year and rising. This was a significant fraction of the $22 billion in gold and international monetary reserves which President Kennedy discovered to be held by the US government in January 1961. Eisenhower's Treasury Secretary had already visited the European central bankers to ask for their restraint, with little success, and it was his deputy, the Republican Douglas Dillon, whom the worried Kennedy appointed to be his own Treasury Secretary. Dillon, whose European credentials and tastes were reflected in his purchase of France's Haut-Brion vineyard, found his efforts frustrated by Kennedy's own economic policies.[11]

Eisenhower had tried, and failed, to balance his budgets, and suffered a $12 billion budget deficit in 1958. Kennedy was a more enthusiastic Keynesian, and in 1961 began a series of fiscal deficits in the federal budget that were to last until 1969. The budget deficit averaged $6 billion a year in the 1960s, until the Vietnam War took it to $25.2 billion in 1968. And America's balance-of-payments deficit on official settlements went from $3.4 billion in 1960 to $10.7 billion in 1970.[12] At Bretton Woods in 1945, the United States had sown the seeds of its own economic crisis by rigging the rules of international currencies to suit itself, and match its economic dominance. But that dominance could not be indefinitely sustained, and by force-feeding the growth of the Japanese and Western European economies, the United States brought the day of reckoning closer. The US economy was so vast and resilient that the harvest was only to be reaped in the 1970s, but throughout the 1960s it was growing and ripening. The Democratic Administrations of 1961–9 financed – all on deficits and on credit – their rearmament boom, their domestic welfare reforms and 'Great Society' programmes, as well as the Vietnam War and their growing private investments in Japan and in Western Europe. It was too much.

Had the US economy kept pace with those whose growth it had financed, the dominance of the post-war years could have been maintained. But during the 1950s, industrial productivity in Germany increased by 6 per cent a year, and in France by 4 per cent. US productivity, by contrast, was growing at 2.4 per cent annually over the decade. This not only implied a relative decline of US economic efficiency, it also became a self-sustaining trend, as US corporations realised they could make better returns on their investment in Europe than at home, and began to export more capital overseas to take advantage of it. In 1950, the book value of US holdings in Europe was $1.7 billion, and by 1969 it had increased more than tenfold to $21.5 billion.[13]

Most of the profits of these American-owned enterprises remained in Europe, to be reinvested, and help swell that astonishing new international currency, the Eurodollar. The Eurodollar was homeless money, the American money which had left the United States and stayed in European banks to become a new financial instrument. By 1966, there were some $15 billion in Eurodollars being traded in the European markets, an uncontrolled currency whose size and volatility helped force the devaluations of the original dollar in the 1970s.[14]

From the traditional US point of view, this was a progression towards national impoverishment. But tradition was a poor guide to the extraordinary transformation which the Cold War was inducing in the American economy. Until 1940, when conscription was first introduced in peacetime, America had always had a tiny standing army. In 1939, it numbered only 174,000 men, and although the US Navy represented a substantial investment, the defence budget took only 3.4 per cent of the GDP. The Cold War changed all that. The Army grew with the special demands of the Korean and Vietnam wars, but even in nominal peacetime, the US Army was maintained at a complement of around one million men, and the share of the overall US economy devoted to defence remained between two and three times the levels of 1939.

The US economy was not only to this degree militarised by the Cold War, it was also internationalised. American patterns of trade and investment were transformed, and what had been a virtually self-sufficient economy before the Second World War became locked ever more deeply into the global trading system that was emerging. The trend is plain. From the depth of the Great Depression in 1933, when total US exports amounted to $1.65 billion, America's trading relationships with the rest of the world simply exploded. A snapshot of US exports at the start of each new decade shows the following (in billion dollars):

1950	1960	1970	1980	1990
$10.2	$20.4	$42.6	$216.7	$421.6

Exports tell but part of the story. The investment by American companies in the Western European economy, and increasingly in Japan too, intensified this trend of the deepening interdependence of the Western world. From a total of $1.7 billion in 1950, to a total of $21.5 billion in 1969, by 1989 this flood of private investment was running at the extraordinary level of $150 billion a year. This was the global economy with a vengeance. And these investments were not made by government strategists or bureaucrats or statesmen as the

Marshall Plan had been, but by wealth-seeking managers and entre-
preneurs. Just as the Cold War had forced the USA to internationalise
its military commitments and spread its bases across the globe, so
trade followed the flag and internationalised the US economy too. The
process also transformed the nature of industrial organisation.

If the classic managerial structure of the first phase of the industrial
revolution in Britain had been the joint stock company, and the next
phase of industrial expansion was led by the cartels of individual
nations, the characteristic formation of the Cold War's global economy was the multinational corporation. By 1968, for example, a mere
twenty US-based corporations accounted for more than two-thirds of
all US investment in Western Europe, and some 40 per cent of US
investments in France, Britain and Germany were held by three
multinationals, Ford, General Motors and Standard Oil of New
Jersey, better known as Exxon.

Seen from Western Europe, two interpretations of this process were
possible. An economic nationalist like President de Gaulle, or his
austere financial adviser Jacques Rueff, could see this as an American
economic invasion, financed on the sly by paper money and an
inflating dollar. Taking the longer view, we can see this as an essential
stage in the building of a global economy. The American balance-of-
payments syndrome became the mechanism by which the wealth of
United States had accumulated during and after World War Two was
redistributed in productive investments elsewhere. The United States
might have hoped to maintain for ever that 50 per cent of global GDP
which it enjoyed in 1946, but the 25 per cent share it was to enjoy by
the 1980s was a smaller share of a vastly larger global economy.
Americans might not have kept pace with the economic growth rates
of Europe and Japan, but they had got very much richer anyway.[15]

This steady shifting of economic weight from the United States to
the European allies it had rescued and financed makes American
strategic policy in the 1960s look like altruism comparable to the
generosity of the Marshall Plan. It was also, of course, done in the
longer-term American national interest. National security, not to say
the verdict of the next US Presidential election, was deemed to hinge
on maintaining the countries of Western Europe as American allies
and trading partners and the areas as a US sphere of influence. But this
national security was not cheaply bought. The United States continued
to devote a far greater share of its wealth than the Europeans to its
defence budget, at least a third of which could be ascribed to Nato.

The US sold cheaply to Britain the technology and equipment necessary to maintain British nuclear pretensions, and later secretly donated nuclear skills to France.[16]

The United States was so lavish with its nuclear weapons that in 1960, while the world and particularly the Soviet Union were constantly assured that West Germany would never become a nuclear power, the Joint Committee on Atomic Energy of the US Congress discovered that this was not so. By accident, in the course of a visit to a Nato airbase in Germany, they discovered German-manned fighter-bombers sitting on alert on the edge of the runway, and equipped with nuclear weapons. The only evidence of the much-vaunted 'American control of warheads' was the presence of a US Air Force officer, equipped with a revolver, 'somewhere in the vicinity'.[17] As a result of this incident, PALs, or Permissive Action Links, to give real control over the warheads, were developed and deployed. Such was the US generosity, and good sense in a hair-trigger nuclear world, that the PAL technology was later made freely available to the Soviet Union by US Defense Secretary Robert McNamara.[18]

This incident on the German airfield took place as the United States was facing the very real possibility of nuclear war with the Soviet Union over Berlin. It was for the West a heroic and beleaguered outpost, and for the Warsaw Pact it was an open sore, through which spies and radio and TV propaganda leaked one way, and East Germany's own best-educated citizens leaked out in the other direction. The tension of the time is caught by Khrushchev's offhand remark to the US Ambassador Llewellyn Thompson at a Kremlin New Year's Eve party at the end of 1960. Talking blithely of the need to avoid nuclear suicide, Khrushchev said that fifty nuclear bombs were assigned to France, 'more than enough to destroy that country'. Another thirty each were allocated to Britain and West Germany. Mrs Thompson asked how many were devoted to the USA. 'That is a secret,' Khrushchev replied.[19]

He may have been joking. One suspects not. The prospect of war was extraordinarily close at the start of the 1960s, and even without nuclear war, the Soviet leader was convinced that the eventual defeat of the West was inevitable. Indeed, two days before President Kennedy was inaugurated, Khrushchev published a truncated version of a speech he had given to party propagandists on 6 January. Nuclear war would destroy civilisation, he said, but the 'sacred struggle of national liberation . . . [was now] . . . the only way of bringing imperialism to heel'. Kennedy had copies of the speech circulated to his top advisers, with the comment 'Read, learn and inwardly digest'.[20] Kennedy's own rhetoric proved even more fiery, and the combination of his inaugural address and his first formal statement to Congress was bluntly bellicose towards Moscow, and deliberately alarmist for his own people and allies.

'We shall pay any price, bear any burden, meet any hardship, support any friend, oppose any foe to ensure the survival and success of liberty,' he declared in the address. The later phrase, 'My fellow Americans, ask not what your country can do for you; ask what you can do for your country', certainly caught the imagination of his fellow countrymen.

In Moscow, the trick was to comprehend which message was being sent to them. Was it the call to talks – 'Let us never negotiate out of fear, but let us never fear to negotiate'? Or was it the following, even more ambiguous clarion call?[21]

> Since this country was founded, each generation of Americans has been summoned to give testimony to its national loyalty. The graves of young Americans who answered the call to service surround the globe. Now the trumpet summons us again – not as a call to bear arms, though arms we need; not as a call to battle, though embattled we are; but a call to bear the burden of a long twilight struggle, year in and year out, rejoicing in hope, patient in tribulation, a struggle against the common enemies of man; tyranny, poverty, disease and war itself.

These were stirring words, high-flown and deliberate oratory which retain a certain magic today. But what do the words actually say? Moscow's bafflement in the face of these balanced but contradictory phrases commands sympathy. The plight of the Central Committee's translators was acute. Doubtless they in the Kremlin were the 'tyranny', identified as the first of the common enemies of man. That was clear. But were they being invited to an international coalition to give foreign aid to the poor, or to a nuclear war? Were the Americans called to arms or not? Were these already embattled Americans being called to a new battlefront, and if so where, and against whom?

Matters were somewhat clarified ten days later, in the second Kennedy address, to the Joint Houses of Congress, although again the penchant of the Presidential speechwriters for the balanced cadences imbued the entire statement with a studied ambiguity. But there was no mistaking the thrust of the message. Now that the new President had looked at the international situation, and at the means he had inherited to cope with it, one conclusion was compelling. The West was losing the Cold War.[22]

No man entering upon this office, regardless of his party, regardless of his previous service in Washington, could fail to be staggered upon learning – even in this brief ten-day period – the harsh enormity of the trials through which we must pass in the next four years. Each day the crises multiply. Each day their solution grows more difficult. Each day we grow nearer the hour of maximum danger, as weapons spread and hostile forces grow stronger. I feel I must inform the Congress that our analyses over the last ten days make it clear that – in each of the principal areas of crisis – the tide of events has been running out, and time has not been our friend.

Kennedy announced a crash programme to bring the new Polaris and Minuteman strategic missiles into operation. Two months later, after a brisk defence review, he announced that the Polaris building programme would be doubled that year, and the increased total of twenty-nine boats, each armed with sixteen nuclear missiles, would start coming from the shipyards at the rate of one a month. The Minuteman production capacity was also doubled, and the B-52 and B-47 nuclear bomber force was to be placed on a crisis footing. Half of the entire force was to be on fifteen-minute alert at any given time.

While this capacity for massive retaliation was being assembled, the doctrine of massive retaliation was itself to be modified: 'Our objective is to increase our capacity to confine our response to non-nuclear weapons.' Accordingly, conventional forces of men and ships and warplanes were to be increased, along with the airlift capacity to deploy them. They would be trained for new battlefields with new quasi-guerrilla tactics and equipment. 'Non-nuclear wars, and sublimited or guerrilla warfare, have since 1945 constituted the most active and constant threat to free world security.'[23]

Between the announcement of 'the hour of maximum danger' and the military responses to it, the crises had brewed. On 13 February, the Soviet Union threatened to intervene in the newly independent Congo, after the assassination of its first leader Patrice Lumumba. The CIA was involved in this, even if the final killing was carried out by Congolese troops. The local CIA station chief, Lawrence Devlin, had in fact been ordered to arrange Lumumba's death, and given a suitable kit of toxins and hypodermic needles.[24] The pro-Communist Pathet Lao were so close to taking control of Laos that 'detailed plans for the introduction of American forces were presented to the President' on 9 March.[25] On 18 March, a nationalist uprising broke out in Angola against the Portuguese colonial regime, a Nato ally. The uprising was, in the words of Kennedy's special counsel Ted Sorensen, 'supported by America's African friends'. On 21 March, at the Geneva talks on a nuclear testing ban, the Soviet negotiators called for a veto over the special inspections being envisaged to verify compliance with the treaty, which the United States saw as ditching the prospects for a test ban.

While the new defence-spending speech was being written, two further crises were gestating. At Baikonur, the Soviet space station, Lieutenant Valentin Bondarenko died in an accidental oxygen fire on 23 March while preparing to become the first man to be launched into space.[26] And in their secret CIA training camps in Guatemala, the 1,400 men of Cuban exile Brigade 2506 were preparing to invade Cuba. The stage was set for another symbolic confrontation, a new Soviet success in space to set against a new American disaster. On 12 April, Yuri Gagarin, who was Lieutenant Bondarenko's first reserve and had stood over his deathbed, more than repeated the triumph and the shock of the Sputnik launch four years earlier. Soviet man had once again paraded his technological prowess, winning the race to orbit the earth, and was quick to trumpet the implications. Said *Pravda*:[27]

> You wish to know what Communism is, gentlemen? Then open your eyes to the heavens and you will see that Labour has become master of a considerable part of the world, and behold what it produces. A Soviet man has left the confines of the earth. This sentence alone, like a mathematical formula, sums up the preceding history of human society, the harnessing of the mighty forces of nature and the growth of man himself.

On the day this *Pravda* editorial appeared, the Cuban exiles landed on Zapata Beach at Cuba's Bay of Pigs. The surprise air-strike by B-26 bombers, provided by the CIA and masquerading as Cuban Air Force defectors, failed to destroy the Cuban fighters on their airfields. The obsolete B-26 bombers were then shot from the sky by the Cuban jet trainer aircraft, who also sank the ammunition supply ship on which the invaders depended. Fidel Castro's army and militia reacted with impressive speed and military skill, and within three days, had killed, captured or thrown off the entire landing force. They had seen themselves as liberators, but the expected popular rising against Castro did not occur. Indeed, the defeat of the US-backed invasion testified to the strength of Castro's popular support.

This was not Kennedy's operation, but an inheritance from Eisenhower. It had been planned since March of the previous year by the

CIA's highly confident covert operations branch under Richard Bissell. Kennedy was personally assured by the CIA chief Allen Dulles that the invasion would succeed in toppling Castro.[28] Kennedy insisted that no US forces be directly involved, although US aircraft were to fly an ill-coordinated air-cover mission, and to help retrieve some of the attackers from the beach.[29] It was a humiliating disaster, fraught with ominous implications for Kennedy's policy towards that developing and newly independent world he had addressed in his inaugural speech. 'We pledge our word that one form of colonial control shall not have passed away merely to be replaced by a far more iron tyranny,' he had said then. And while his meaning is clear, the Bay of Pigs was an unhappy way to go about it. The concern the defeat aroused among America's allies about the future US role in the developing world was regretfully expressed by *Le Monde*: 'Soviet propaganda will find it easy to convince world opinion, starting with the peoples of Latin America, Africa and Asia, that the vaunted anti-colonialism of the USA is no more than a façade which shelters a hypocritical idealism.'[30]

The Soviet Union was, in fact, drawing a rather different lesson. Still flushed with Gagarin's space triumph, *Pravda* noted: 'The time has passed forever when the US could brandish its stick in the belief that it was the biggest and longest, because the other side now has equally long and heavy, and no less powerful sticks.'[31]

The reaction of the world's press to the Bay of Pigs is instructive, in part because this was an audience in which Kennedy took great interest, believing that the Cold War was ultimately a struggle for the hearts and minds of people across the globe. The massed editorials, and the role of the US press in particular, also reveal the degree to which the media felt it was part of the struggle. The *New York Times* and the *Washington Post* both knew of the invasion in advance, as they had known of the U-2 spy flights over the Soviet Union, and held back their stories in the national interest. At the request of the CIA, the *New York Times* withdrew its reporter from Guatemala, which at least saved him the embarrassment of being on the scene of a story which would not be run. Phil Graham, publisher of the *Post* and a friend of Kennedy, even 'killed' a critical editorial on the eve of the invasion.[32]

There was no doubt whose side the newspapers were on. 'The struggle now going on for Cuba is like a battle in a long, complicated and spread-out war . . . The US is engaged in an all-out struggle to save the Western Hemisphere for democracy and freedom,' ran the *New York Times* editorial. But this was already more than a regional or hemispheric issue. Khrushchev in Moscow had warned: 'We shall render the Cuban people all necessary assistance in beating back the armed aggression against them.' The *Washington Post* was supportive of the White House, but depressed by the implications of failure: 'If now the invasion should fail, it would appear to the world as if the Soviet Union had saved [its] Cuban stooges by intimidating the United States. That is the unlovely prospect that may confront this country unless the effort to deliver Cuba from the Communists quickly catches hold.'[33]

Equally interesting is the degree to which the leading papers of the European allies echoed this reflex support of the American position. West Germany's conservative *Die Welt* strained to see the entire affair as a Western victory: 'The unmistakable "Halt" which the young President has conveyed to Khrushchev leaves no more doubt about American policy towards the USSR and its lust to expand. The USSR is fully answered, in the proper form, in an unshakeable manner.' And Italy's *Corriere della sera* openly mourned: 'This failure is a tragedy. A tragedy for that courageous band of men who went to fight against a bloody tyranny and who are now, in part, its prisoners.'[34]

This media support was in sharp contrast to the wave of anti-American demonstrations across Latin America, and the stoning of the US Embassies in Tokyo, New Delhi and Cairo. The goodwill which Kennedy had sought to build in the developing world with his promises of more aid programmes and the Peace Corps was seriously jeopardised. The reaction was particularly severe in Latin America, which Kennedy liked to call 'our sister republics south of our border', and which had the previous month been promised an Alliance for Progress: a commitment to $20 billion in US aid over the next ten years. Generous in view of the balance-of-payments pressure on Kennedy's Treasury, this was strategically an indispensable investment if it could buy off the seductions of Cuba, the first socialist outpost in the western hemisphere.

'The great battleground for the defence and expansion of freedom today is Asia, Africa and the Middle East, the lands of the rising peoples,' the President told Congress just a month after the invasion's defeat.

> The adversaries of freedom did not create the revolution, but they are seeking to ride the crest of its wave, to capture it for themselves. Yet their aggression is more often concealed than open. They have fired no missiles, and their troops are seldom seen. They send arms, agitators, aid, technicians and propaganda to every troubled area. But where fighting is required, it is usually done by others, by guerillas striking at